The Meaning of Repentance

The MEANING of REPENTANCE

WILLIAM DOUGLAS CHAMBERLAIN
Professor of New Testament Exegesis
Louisville Presbyterian Seminary

WIPF & STOCK · Eugene, Oregon

Wipf and Stock Publishers
199 W 8th Ave, Suite 3
Eugene, OR 97401

The Meaning of Repentance
By Chamberlain, William Douglas
ISBN 13: 978-1-5326-4576-1
Publication date 12/12/2017
Previously published by The Westminster Press, 1943

To My Students

PREFACE

The contents of this volume consist largely of the Smyth Lectures delivered at Columbia Theological Seminary, 1941. Chapters III and VI have been completely rewritten and there has been some revision in each of the other four.

The conclusions stated in these chapters have grown out of firsthand investigation of the materials lying in the twenty-seven " canonical books " of the New Testament. The method pursued has been to study the New Testament directly, rather than to read what others say about it. It is an increasingly strong conviction with me that we as ministers have not done enough of this kind of study.

Reference to the various theories of authorship, date, and provenance of the " books " has been studiously avoided, for the simple reason that I wanted to examine the New Testament as a body of writings expressing the convictions and faith of the Early Church. It is interesting, however, that the theory of *Formgeschichte*, as advocated by Dibelius,[1] represents Jesus as inaugurating his ministry with the preaching of " repentance ": " Now after John was cast into prison, Jesus appeared in Galilee and proclaimed the Message of God: ' The time is fulfilled, the kingdom of God is at hand; repent and believe in the Message of Salvation.'"

It is also worth noting that II Peter, the writing of which is placed by many scholars near the middle of the second century, represents " repentance " as having an important place in the plan of God: " The Lord is not slack concerning his promise, as some count slackness; but is longsuffering to you-ward, not wishing that any should perish, but that all should come to repentance." So, if we follow the conclusions of the critical scholars, we find the New Testament message opening and closing on the note of repentance. If we follow the beaten path of conservative scholarship, we find the same note of repentance opening and closing the New Testament. From either approach the New Testament is essentially a unit on this theme.

I desire to thank President J. McDowell Richards, the faculty and the students of Columbia Theological Seminary for a week of delightful fellowship in their midst. I owe a great debt to Mrs. Chamberlain who helped to revise the manuscript in lecture form and later for publication. She also prepared the Table of Contents, the Index of Scripture References, and the typescript. My thanks are also due to Mrs. N. A. McCawley, who typed one draft of the lectures.

I wish to express appreciation for permission to quote to the following: The Macmillan Company,

God Who Speaks, by Burnett H. Streeter, and *A Preface to Christian Theology,* by John A. Mackay; The Westminster Press, *Institutes of the Christian Religion,* by John Calvin.

WILLIAM DOUGLAS CHAMBERLAIN

Louisville Presbyterian Seminary,
March, 1943.

TABLE OF CONTENTS

I

THE NEED FOR A RESTUDY OF REPENTANCE	15
The Reason for the Need	17
The Causes of the Misunderstanding	27
The Protest	35

II

THE NEW TESTAMENT EMPHASIS ON REPENTANCE	51
John the Baptist's Preaching	51
Jesus' Preaching	54
Jesus' Instructions	56
God's Eternal Purpose	59
The Apostles' Preaching	61
Peter's Emphasis	62
Paul's Emphasis	66
The Epistles of Paul	70
The Epistle to the Hebrews	72
The General Epistles	74
The Apocalypse	77
Conclusion	80

III

THE IMPLICATIONS OF REPENTANCE	83
God	84
Man	91
What God Expects of Man	104
The Nature of the Kingdom	115

IV

THE TWO MINDS: THE MIND OF THE FLESH AND THE MIND OF CHRIST — 127
The Conflict Between the Two Minds — 127
The Mind of the Flesh — 134
The Mind of Christ — 141
The Transition Is Repentance — 143
The Reorientation of the Mind of Man — 148

V

HOW REPENTANCE IS PRODUCED — 159
How Repentance Is Not Produced — 160
    Fear or Intimidation — 160
    Increased Evidence — 162
    Sorrow for Sin — 164
How Repentance Is Produced — 171
    The Work of the Holy Spirit — 172
    The Participation of the Human Will — 184
    The Powers of the New Mind — 188

VI

THE MEANING OF THESE THINGS FOR PREACHING — 193
The Primacy of Preaching — 204
    Getting the Materials — 207
    Using the Materials — 217
Summary — 222
NOTES — 227
INDEX OF SCRIPTURE REFERENCES — 233

For my thoughts are not yet your thoughts, neither are your ways my ways, saith Jehovah. — Isa. 55:8.

1

THE NEED FOR A RESTUDY OF REPENTANCE

The New Testament opens with a trumpet blast: "Repent ye; for the kingdom of heaven is at hand" (Matt. 3:2). These are the first words recorded from the lips of John the Baptist. Mark does not give the exact words of John, but he does say that he preached "the baptism of repentance unto remission of sins" (Mark 1:4). Matthew (Matt. 4:17) records that Jesus also initiated his ministry with the words, "Repent ye; for the kingdom of heaven is at hand." In this respect, John and Jesus issued identical challenges to their generation.

Since both John and Jesus probably preached in Aramaic, the question arises, Does the Greek word translated "repent" correctly represent the word they used, which is lost to us? There are four possible avenues through which to seek light.

1. The various efforts to recover the Aramaic "behind" the Gospels are not yet sufficiently successful to answer this question satisfactorily.
2. The Syriac translations of the Gospels might

help; they render the Greek word "turn ye." But there is a general lack of nicety in translating synonyms into the Syriac versions, so it is dangerous to presume too much on the Syriac word "turn ye."

3. The prophets used "turn ye" in their preaching. It is true that Jesus was in line with the prophets in much of his preaching, but he also went beyond them in his insights. Could he not have used a word deeper in meaning than that of the prophets?

4. New Testament usage suggests that he did. If Jesus had said, "Turn ye," the most natural translation would have been ἐπιστρέφω, which frequently occurs in the New Testament in the sense of reformation of conduct, conversion, and reconciliation. Luke (Luke 22:32) uses this word in reporting Jesus' conversation concerning Peter's turning again after his sifting. If Jesus had said, "Turn ye; for the kingdom of heaven is at hand," ἐπιστρέφω would have been the obvious word for the Evangelists to use. But there is no faltering or divided testimony among the Synoptists: all record that Jesus called for a change of mind. The Gospel of John calls for a rebirth, a new nature in Nicodemus. This fact is further evidence that Jesus used some

The Need for a Restudy

word which the New Testament writers felt could be properly translated only by a word describing a change of nature, a new mind.

This formula, "Repent ye; for the kingdom of heaven is at hand," is not only a trumpet blast, but also the keynote of the New Testament message. Not only does it break the stillness of the Judean wilderness, but its reverberations are heard throughout the New Testament, reaching their climax in the thunders of the Apocalypse.

If these words do constitute the keynote, we must understand them before we understand the New Testament. Since the faith of the Christian rests chiefly upon the New Testament, that faith will be either foggy or crystal-clear, in proportion as it grasps its great, essential teachings. Intelligent, consistent Christian living is inseparable from the basic ideas of the Christian faith. Revelation, response; doctrine, life can be separated conceptually, but in practical life they are linked by vital bonds.

The Reason for the Need

The Church has not understood the words, "Repent ye," in their profound, far-reaching, revolutionary significance. John A. Broadus has called this the "worst translation in the New Testament."[2] The result has been that the popular concept of repentance has been tragically shallow: it has been perverted into emotionalism or sacramentarianism. Having misunderstood the primary demand of the Christian faith, the Church has failed to be the force in the world that it should be. The most devastating wars of the modern world have usually broken out between so-called Christian nations. This of itself indicates that there is something radically wrong with Christianity as we practice it.

It is supremely important that we understand this doctrine as we look ahead to rebuilding civilization. It will do little good to "win the war," if we go on doing the things that provoke wars. Scientific and industrial achievement will make each succeeding war more terrible than its predecessor, unless we learn how to live together. The New Testament idea of repentance offers the solution. The providence of God is opening for us a door of opportunity to present the remedy to the world.

The scope of the misunderstanding of repentance has been as wide as Western Christianity. This has been true of both Protestantism and Catholicism. I do not mean that no Christians have grasped the meaning of Jesus' message, "Repent ye." I do mean to say that the mass of Christians have not risen, even approximately, to the level of Jesus' meaning.

In the Protestant Church, for instance, repentance

The Need for a Restudy

has been almost exclusively associated with an emotional crisis of sorrow for sin and fear of punishment. There has developed in the minds of our more intelligent people a mental resistance to the idea of repentance as they have heard it preached. The instinct back of this reaction is essentially sound. The popular evangelist has so frequently used the fear of punishment to precipitate this crisis, that, in the minds of many, the word repent veritably smells of fire and brimstone. Hell is not the vivid reality that it once was. The hell of the high-pressure evangelist has seldom been Biblical, but is rather Miltonic, or sub-Miltonic. There is a crying need for the preaching of repentance today, but we must put it on a Biblical basis. When we do, men will listen.

The reason which John and Jesus both give for repentance is *not* that the Kingdom of heaven *may* come near, but that it *has* drawn near. Repentance does not bring the Kingdom; it prepares men to participate in it. Repentance is not a device for escaping hell; it is a preparation for co-operating with God's will on earth. John follows his challenge with the command:

" Prepare ye the way of the Lord,
Make his paths straight " (Matt. 3:3).

Jesus followed his by: "Come ye after me, and I will make you fishers of men " (Matt. 4:19).

Both Jesus and John offer men opportunities for

service to the Messiah: preparing a way for his progress or winning men to his leadership. It is true that John said later, according to the narrative, " Ye offspring of vipers, who warned you to flee from the wrath to come? " (Luke 3:7.) There is the threat of judgment here, but it is secondary to the invitation to service. In Jesus' teaching, also, there are references to judgment, but they are made only after men have rejected an invitation — for example, to a wedding feast. It is then that Jesus speaks of " outer darkness," of " the weeping and the gnashing of teeth " (Matt. 22:1–14).

Jesus offered citizenship in the Kingdom, not the menace of hell, as the motive for repentance. These two approaches represent radically different conceptions of religion. Robert Burns expressed the difference in his " Epistle to a Young Friend ":

" The fear o' hell's a hangman's whip
    To haud the wretch in order;
But where ye feel your honour grip,
    Let that aye be your border."

The Christian is not a man driven to do right by fear of a scourge; the Christian is motivated by the Spirit of God within. When Jesus preached repentance, he offered opportunities for service; his followers have often coupled repentance with threats of damnation. We must face the question today as to

The Need for a Restudy

which is *the* evangel. Which type of preaching is most needed in our day? Jesus said, "Come ye after me, and I will make you fishers of men." To hear some of Jesus' followers, one would think he said, "Follow me or you will go to hell." The important thing to notice is where Jesus placed the accent in his preaching.

In the Roman Church, repentance is circumscribed by the idea of doing penance, i.e., to making satisfaction for particular sins committed. A modern Catholic writer [3] seems to state the position of that Church better than I can. Beginning with Clement of Rome, the earliest of the Apostolic Fathers, he traces the idea of μετάνοια through the rest of the Apostolic Fathers, the Apologists, the Reformers, and modern writers, both Catholic and Protestant. He correctly finds the roots of the idea in the Old Testament idea of conversion from sin. He finds, in Clement and later Catholic writers, the assumption that repentance implies (*a*) contrition for sin, (*b*) confession, (*c*) amendment, and (*d*) satisfaction by means of penitential works.[4] He assumes that Clement and all his successors in the Catholic tradition had the New Testament idea of repentance; and then uses their views to interpret the New Testament. The Reformers, he thinks, went astray in returning to the etymological sense, "Change your mind."[5] He does not understand the full depth of meaning which Calvin, for instance, would put into the word. The difference in the two views lies in the fact that the Reformers place the emphasis on the transformation of the whole mind, heart, and will of man, while the Catholic view tends to leave the emphasis on the penitential practices of the sinner seeking pardon. In the latter view, the woods cannot be seen for the trees: men lose their sense of sin in their preoccupation with sins. This restricts repentance to particulars, when it was intended that it should touch every phase of life, thought, and aspiration.

Men have lost their moral perspective, in both the Protestant and Catholic communions. Sin has become more a matter of actions than of attitude. One's attitude is the expression of one's bent or tendency of mind. A wrong attitude toward God and man leads to wrong actions toward both God and man. A transformation of the mind transforms the man; a transformation of the man transforms his conduct.

The great weakness in these popular views is that they turn the Christian's gaze backward rather than forward. The Christian faith turns men's faces forward. Repentance is the reorientation of a personality with reference to God and his purpose.

Calvin deals with some of the inadequate notions of repentance: " In the first place, the definition they have given of repentance, clearly shows that they

The Need for a Restudy 23

never understood what it was; for they catch at some passages in the writings of the fathers, which by no means express the nature of repentance; as, 'that to repent is to weep for sins previously committed, and not to commit sins to be wept for.' Again: 'that it is to lament evils that are past, and not to commit new ones to be lamented.' Again: 'that it is a kind of mournful vengeance, punishing in ourselves what we bewail having committed.' Again: 'that it is a sorrow of heart and bitterness of soul on account of the evils which a man has committed, or to which he has consented.'"[6]

Again, Calvin says: "As this of Chrysostom, 'Repentance is a medicine which destroys sin, a gift bestowed from heaven, an admirable virtue, a grace exceeding the power of laws.' Moreover, the doctrine which they afterwards advance is still worse than these definitions; for they are so obstinately riveted to external exercises, that one can collect nothing else from immense volumes, but that repentance is an austere discipline, which serves partly to subdue the flesh, partly to chastise and punish vices; but concerning the internal renovation of the mind, which is attended with a real reformation of the life, they observe a wonderful silence. Of *contrition* and *attrition*, indeed, they treat largely; they torment souls with a multitude of scruples, and drive them to extreme trouble and anxiety; but when they appear to have thoroughly wounded the heart, they heal all the bitterness by a slight sprinkling of ceremonies."[7]

Although Calvin was thinking primarily of the Roman Church, the same criticism might, with equal truth, be made of much Protestant thinking on repentance, e.g., "Repentance is being sorry for your sins — so sorry that you won't commit them again." How often one reads or hears some such definition as this for repentance! I must confess to having used it myself on numerous occasions, before I began to see the profound depths in the New Testament teaching on this subject.

At best, both in Protestant and in Roman Catholic churches, repentance has meant, in the popular mind, simply godly sorrow for sin. This statement is not intended as a criticism of those devout Christians who have not fully understood Jesus' meaning. We should not feel critical toward such Christians; rather, we should thank God for Christian faith wherever we find it, recognizing that our own exhibit of the Christian faith has many and serious flaws in it. It is, however, a fair assumption that the sincere Christian is always ready to acknowledge incompleteness of understanding and inconsistency in practice. Honesty is an essential part of Christian experience.

That repentance includes more than godly sorrow

The Need for a Restudy

for sin is clearly taught by the Apostle Paul. He draws a sharp distinction between the two in the following words: " For though I made you sorry with my epistle, I do not regret it: though I did regret it (for I see that that epistle made you sorry, though but for a season), I now rejoice, not that ye were made sorry, but that ye were made sorry unto repentance; for ye were made sorry after a godly sort, that ye might suffer loss by us in nothing. For godly sorrow worketh repentance unto salvation, a repentance which bringeth no regret: but the sorrow of the world worketh death " (II Cor. 7:8–10). A good example of the latter is Judas Iscariot, who, conscious of his guilt, cried, " I have sinned in that I betrayed innocent blood " (Matt. 27:4), and then went out and hanged himself.

Godly sorrow may lead to repentance, but is in no sense identical with it. It is at this point that Western Christianity has missed a primary emphasis of the New Testament. As already suggested, John Calvin vigorously protested against the notion that repentance is primarily a matter of mourning and lamenting sins: " But as some persons . . . consider fasting and weeping as the principal part of repentance, their mistake requires to be rectified." [8]

This misconception of repentance has colored most of the devotional books of the Church. It has produced such extremes of self-torture as those of the Penitentes of our own Southwest; it has produced the pious morbidity of a Kierkegaard. Self-torture, whether the body or the spirit be the victim, does not produce the New Testament type of piety. Kierkegaard,[9] a man of great spiritual stature, considered it his duty to spend the remainder of his life mourning over the sins of his youth. He never realized that, when God had removed his sins " as far as the east is from the west," he too should cease to make their consideration the primary occupation of his life. He spent his whole life prying into the motives of his soul. His morbidly morose piety drove many men from religion. This is not the " fruits worthy of repentance " (Luke 3:8) of which the New Testament speaks. Had his intense moral earnestness been directed toward proclaiming the New Testament concept of repentance, he might have made a far more profound impression on his generation. As it was, he was largely ignored until the Barthian movement.

The type of piety epitomized by Kierkegaard has been found in many lands, in many communions, and throughout most of the history of the Church. It keeps a man's attention riveted upon himself, a very small and unworthy preoccupation. Probably the Apostle Paul was more acutely conscious of his early sins than was any other New Testament writer, for

The Need for a Restudy

he refers repeatedly to his career as a persecutor of the Church. He thinks of himself as the very least of the apostles, not worthy to be called an apostle, because he had persecuted the Church (I Cor. 15:9), but he can also, as an old man in prison, broken by his labors, shout, "Rejoice in the Lord always: again I will say, Rejoice" (Phil. 4:4). There was nothing morbid about Paul; the note of joy is struck repeatedly in the midst of trial and hardship. Paul is the best example in the New Testament of what repentance *demands* of one and what it *does* in one.

The Causes of the Misunderstanding

There are three basic causes for the present misunderstanding. The first lies in the mistranslation of "repent," μετανοέω, and "repentance," μετάνοια. This began about A.D. 150, when the New Testament was first translated into Latin. Jesus' challenge was rendered, "*Poenitentiam agite*," "Do penance." This bound the mind of the Latin Church to the penalty connected with sin. Jerome's "revised version," the Vulgate, perpetuated this inadequate translation, and so, in time, the Church began to think of so many acts of penitence to cancel a given amount of sin. To repeat, man became concerned with sins and lost the meaning of sin. The Church also lost sight of the remedy for sin. In doing penance the accent was placed on what *man* did about sin; what *God* had done was obscured and almost forgotten, so far as practical Christian living was concerned.

The English versions, except for the Geneva Bible, followed the Latin rather than the original Greek; so we find Wycliffe [10] rendering the words of Jesus, "Do ye penaunce: for the kingdom of hevens schal come nygh." It should be kept in mind that Wycliffe translated directly from the Vulgate, that he knew no Greek, and that he probably never saw a Greek manuscript of the New Testament.

William Tyndale [11] was capable of translating directly from the Greek, but he followed the Vulgate in this case. He improved, however, on Wycliffe, rendering Jesus' words, "Repent ye, for the kingdome of heven is at honde." But he was held by the leading strings of a mistranslation. "Repent" brings out the idea of afterthought on sin. The thought direction is still wrong. As has been said, Jesus called for men to look forward; the translations have been calling on men to look backward. Cranmer,[12] the Authorized Version,[13] the American Standard Version,[14] and others have followed suit with essentially the same words as Tyndale's. The Rheims version of the New Testament,[15] the authorized English version of the Roman Catholic Church, goes back to Wycliffe verbatim, ex-

The Need for a Restudy

cept in spelling: "Do penance for the kingdom of heaven is at hand." Consequently, the English-speaking Roman Catholic still thinks of repentance in terms of " doing penance," making satisfaction for particular sins committed in the past. A Catholic translation, published in 1941, has adopted " Repent, for the kingdom of heaven is at hand," thus continuing the Protestant error.

Nearly all European translations have followed the Vulgate. Martin Luther translated, "*Thut Busse, das Himmelreich ist nähe herbey gekommen*," and so German Protestants still read " Do penance " in their mother tongue. The older French [16] followed the beaten track with "*Repentez-vous*," as did also the Spanish [17] with "*Arrepentíos*," i.e., " Repent," rue, regret your sins. So German, French, Spanish, and English Christians had Jesus' challenge presented to them in the form of, " Rue your sins," regret them, mourn over them.

These infelicitous translations have caused much of European and American Christianity to chant its faith in the wrong key: regret, remorse, and morbid introspection have been regarded as characteristics of true piety. Jesus called for renovation of mind. Traditional piety has often been gloomy; Christian piety should be glad. It has often been felt that if one were sufficiently gloomy, one must be quite saintly. Gloom may simply be an evidence of unconfessed sin. The man who has confessed his sin is a singing man, even though his sin is ever before him as a haunting specter. This was the faith of the psalmist; it should be the faith of the Christian.

A second cause for popular confusion as to the significance of repentance lies in the failure to distinguish, in translation, between the New Testament words μετανοέω and μεταμέλομαι. These two words have entirely different associations in the New Testament, but they are treated as equivalents by our translators. Many devout Christians of my personal acquaintance have been sincerely perplexed as to why thousands repented and were baptized (Acts 2:37-41) on Pentecost, but Judas repented and hanged himself (Matt. 27:3-5). They sense that baptism seems to be regarded as a proper consequence of repentance in one instance, while suicide was equally appropriate in the other. "Why," they say, "was Judas' repentance not accepted? Did not Peter deny his Lord, and was not he forgiven? Why was Judas not forgiven?" I have heard many answers given to these questions, but the true answer lies in the two words that are translated "repent." This is not a mere quibble about words and syllables; it is something vital to a clear understanding of the Christian faith.

The word used of Judas' repentance, μεταμέλομαι,

The Need for a Restudy

refers primarily to "regret or sorrow for what has been done"; the word that is used of Christian repentance, μετανοέω, marks a complete change in mental outlook and of life design. This distinction is disputed on the ground that it was not always so in classical Greek. It is true also that the Septuagint made no clear distinction between these two words, but neither classical Greek nor the Septuagint can be taken as the criterion for New Testament Greek.

There are certain marked and indisputable differences in these two words in the New Testament: the first and most obvious being frequency of use. The verb, μετανοέω, used in Jesus' challenge, occurs in the New Testament thirty-four times; its cognate noun, μετάνοια, occurs twenty-two times; making a total of fifty-six occurrences. The verb that is used of Judas' repentance, μεταμέλομαι, occurs a total of five times; with no instances of its cognate noun, μεταμέλεια. So, the score is fifty-six to five for the two word groups. Obviously, then, when one thinks of "repentance" in the New Testament, it must be in terms of μετανοέω.

In terms of etymology, also, there is a difference. The word used of Judas means to "have care afterward," to experience regret or remorse. The term used of Christian repentance has been taken in the sense of "afterthought," i.e., afterthought on sin, but μετά in compounds can mean "trans" as well as "post." The meaning "trans," rather than "post," fits the New Testament usage, i.e., "Reverse your thoughts." George Campbell, of Aberdeen, in his *Preliminary Dissertations*[18] (1788), says, μετανοέω "marks a change of mind that is durable and productive of consequences," while μεταμέλομαι "expresses only a present uneasy feeling of regret or sorrow for what is done, without regard either to duration or to effects." "The first," he says, "may be properly translated into English, 'I reform'; the second, 'I repent,' in the familiar acceptation of the word."

Grotius[19] objected to this distinction on the grounds of two New Testament passages. The first passage cited by Grotius is in the parable of the Two Sons. The son who answered, "I will not: but afterward he repented himself [μεταμεληθείς], and went" (Matt. 21:29), is said to have changed his conduct. To this, Campbell replied: "The change as far as it went was a real reformation. Everyone who reforms, repents; but everyone who repents, does not reform. . . . The genus includes the species, not the species the genus."[20] It might be said further that there is no evidence of any real change in the son who refused to work in the vineyard at his father's request. He may have merely been ashamed of himself. When in a surly mood again, he might well have said, "I will not." Shame at his disobedience might have been the moving factor in his obedience. Was it a grudging obedience?

The Need for a Restudy

The other passage cited by Grotius, Heb. 12:17, seems to argue for a distinction between the words: When Esau, having sold his birthright for a mess of pottage, "afterward desired to inherit the blessing, he was rejected; for he found no place for a change of mind in his father ["in his father" is put in italics by the R.V. because it is not in the Greek], though he sought it diligently with tears." There is plenty of sorrow and regret in this scene, as is evidenced by Esau's tears, and by the fact that Isaac "trembled very exceedingly" (Gen. 27:33). If the revisers are right in referring the "change of mind" to Isaac, the writer of Hebrews draws a sharp distinction between the perturbation of a father over the frivolous disposal of his birthright by his eldest and favorite son and the "change of mind" that Esau requested when he realized what a mistake he had made. If one could be so daring as to refer the phrase "no place of repentance," "change of mind," to Esau, we have the picture of a man weeping and protesting over the loss of a blessing caused by his own appetites, but with those appetites unchanged; so, had opportunity offered again, the birthright might have been sold again for physical gratification.

Clearly there is a sharp distinction between μετανοέω and μεταμέλομαι in the New Testament. Paul brings it out quite decisively in II Cor. 7:8–10, to which attention has already been called: "For though I made you sorry with my epistle, I do not regret it: though I did regret it (for I see that that epistle made you sorry, though but for a season), I now rejoice, not that ye were made sorry, but that ye were made sorry unto repentance; for ye were made sorry after a godly sort, that ye might suffer loss by us in nothing. For godly sorrow worketh repentance unto salvation, a repentance which bringeth no regret: but the sorrow of the world worketh death." In fact, the relations between sorrow, repentance, and regret are all beautifully illustrated in this passage. Godly sorrow leads to " repentance "; the sorrow of the world leads to death. Repentance, μετάνοια, is not only *not* regret, μεταμέλεια, but it is never regretted, ἀμεταμέλητον. The failure to distinguish between these words has confused many Christians, but the great tragedy has been the wrong associations clustering around the typical New Testament word μετανοέω.

A third ground of confusion lies in Old Testament usage. There are, in the Old Testament as in the New, two word groups which are rendered " repent " or " repentance." As in the New Testament, one word has the field almost to itself. *Naham*, נָחַם, " to be penitent," " to be comforted," " to be eased," is used thirty-three times. Of these, thirty refer to God. They seem to designate a change of purpose or procedure on the part of God — an anthropomorphism.

The Need for a Restudy

Three instances only refer to man, and of these but two (Job 42:6; Jer. 8:6) have to do with sorrow for sin. With the associations that, at present, cluster around the word "repent," many Christians are bothered when God is spoken of as "repenting." The other word, *shuv*, שׁוּב, "turn," occurs only three times in the sense of "repent": I Kings 8:47 and Ezek. 14:6; 18:30. It always indicates a change of conduct on the part of man. It comes nearer to expressing the New Testament idea of repentance than the word which is translated "repent."

The Protest

The misunderstanding of the Christian doctrine began with a mistranslation, as I have said, at about the middle of the second century. The protest against this misunderstanding began within a generation. So far as we know, Tertullian was the first to raise his voice in protest: "Now in Greek the word for repentance ($\mu\epsilon\tau\acute{a}\nu o\iota a$) is formed, not from the confession of a sin, but from a change of mind."[21] It is true that here Tertullian is explaining what the Old Testament means when it speaks of the "repentance" of God, but it is also true that he has given the correct etymology of the word "repent," reversal of mind. That Tertullian realized something of the deeper meaning of this is seen in the following statement: "Having found 'the truth,' repent of errors; repent of having loved what God loves not: even we ourselves do not permit our slave-lads not to hate the things which are offensive to us; for the principle of voluntary obedience consists in similarity of minds." [22]

Here, Tertullian strikes the vital spot of the New Testament faith: similarity of mind between God and his people. The thoughts of man are not the thoughts of God, but, before men can enter God's Kingdom, they must be. That is what John and Jesus meant when they proclaimed, "Repent ye; for the kingdom of heaven is at hand." The principle of voluntary obedience in the Kingdom rests on similarity of mind between God and his people. One may mourn over his sins and still be "of the earth, earthy." Morbid introspection is not regeneration. This has its bearing on the doctrine of reconciliation and will be discussed later.

Lactantius (A.D. 260–330) said,[23] "For he who repents of that which he has done, *understands* his former error; and on this account the Greeks better and more significantly speak of $\mu\epsilon\tau\acute{a}\nu o\iota a$, which we may speak of in Latin as 'a return to a right understanding.'"[24] Repentance, then, to Lactantius was a "recovery of one's mind," a return to a mind unperverted by sin.

Theodore Beza took up this suggestion by Lactantius and urged that it be substituted for "*Poenitentiam agite,*" "Do penance." While "recovery of mind," return to sanity, is not a perfect rendering of the Greek, it does remind us that the problem is deeper than mere conduct. It is reminiscent of the Prodigal Son, who "came to himself." The man had a wrong mental bent which must be corrected before he could say, "I will arise and go to my father, and will say unto him, Father, I have sinned against heaven, and in thy sight: I am no more worthy to be called thy son: make me as one of thy hired servants" (Luke 15:18, 19).

This son had experienced a mental metamorphosis: not long before, he had demanded of his father, "Give me the portion of thy substance that falleth to me" (Luke 15:12), and then, with a light heart and an unaccusing conscience, sought the far country to squander what the father had given. The verb "give" is the aorist imperative, the most urgent form of the verb. Before he came to himself, the prodigal was very demanding: he rudely said, "Give me!" Recovering his sanity, he said, "I am not fit to be called thy son." There was more than shame or regret here. This man had come to a new realization of his relationship to the Father. He saw himself and God in a new light. This is repentance.

The Reformers sensed that the significance of Jesus' words had been lost in translation, so, in the Geneva version of the New Testament, they rendered them by, "Amend your lyves."[25] They were getting at the fact that repentance should carry with it a reformation of conduct, as John had insisted when he said, "Bring forth therefore fruits worthy of repentance" (Luke 3:8). The Geneva Bible stood alone among the versions in its independence; but it is still inadequate, for it left the impression that repentance is identical with reformation of conduct. This is too shallow. There may be a reformation of conduct without touching the springs of conduct, the mind.

John Calvin went to the heart of the matter when he defined repentance as a "change of mind and intention,"[26] as the laying aside of our old mind and the assuming of a new one. In other words, it is the change of the life design: the whole life pattern is changed; the goal of life is different; the aspirations are different. Calvin said further, "In one word I apprehend repentance to be regeneration, the end of which is the restoration of the Divine image within us; which was defaced, and almost obliterated, by the transgression of Adam."[27] From this point of view, repentance is the making of the new man. In the words of Paul, "If any man is in Christ, he is a new creature" (II Cor. 5:17).

Calvin insisted also that repentance is not an emo-

The Need for a Restudy

tional crisis of fasting and weeping [28] which "terminates within the limits of a few short days," but that it ought to extend throughout the whole of a Christian's life.[29] This is borne out by the fact that both John the Baptist and Jesus are quoted as using the present imperative, μετανοεῖτε. This "transmentation" of the Christian is a progressing, continuing thing: it is not accomplished by an emotional leap. It is a life discipline. To cap off the contribution of Calvin to this discussion, we should note his words: "The substance of the gospel is, not without reason, said to be comprised in 'repentance and remission of sins.'"[30]

Calvin's was not the last voice raised in protest against a misunderstanding of the New Testament idea of repentance. Jeremy Taylor, the greatest Anglican bishop of the seventeenth century, protested vigorously against the misunderstanding of these things in the Church. He called the rendering in the Rheims New Testament, "Do penance," an "absurd reddition" (rendition).[31] He rejected emphatically Erasmus' definition to be "wiser next time; to choose, and to choose better." Erasmus' definition, like hosts of others, conceived of repentance as dealing largely with the past. As Jesus and John presented it, it is a preparation for the future, for the coming Kingdom.

Again, Bishop Taylor said, "To repent is to 'turn'

from darkness to light, from the power of Satan to God, doing works worthy of amendment of life, for the forgiveness of sins, that we may receive inheritance among them that are sanctified by faith in Christ Jesus." [32]

To return to the Old Testament, this idea of the reversal of one's relationships is brought out by the word "turn" or "return": [33] "Return ye, and turn yourselves from your idols; and turn away your faces from all your abominations" (Ezek. 14:6). Peter linked this Old Testament idea with repentance in his discourse on Solomon's porch: "Repent ye therefore, and turn again, that your sins may be blotted out, that so there may come seasons of refreshing from the presence of the Lord; and that he may send the Christ who hath been appointed for you, even Jesus" (Acts 3:19, 20). This correctly emphasizes repentance as a preparation for the future, rather than a mourning over the past.

Jeremy Taylor, in comparing and contrasting these words, referred to "godly sorrow" as the "porch," or the vestibule, of repentance. "Sorrow, and revenge, and holy purposes and protestations, are but single acts of a returning and penitent man: whereas repentance ($\mu\epsilon\tau\acute{a}\nu o\iota a$) is a whole state of a new life, an entire change of the sinner, with all its appendages and instruments of ministry." [34]

The Need for a Restudy

As said before, George Campbell suggested "reform" and "reformation" as translations for μετανοέω and μετάνοια. His objection to leaving the words "repent" and "repentance" in our translations was that the common people do not know of the theological definitions which serve as a corrective for a misleading translation.[35]

He said, further: "I have another objection to the word 'repent.' It unavoidably appears to lay the principal stress on the sorrow or remorse which it implies for former misconduct. Now this appears a secondary matter, at most, and not the idea suggested by the Greek verb. The primary object is a real change of conduct."[36]

The objection to laying the stress on "change of conduct" or "reformation" is that we tend to lead the minds of people away from the fact that μετανοέω deals primarily with the "springs of action," rather than with the actions themselves. Μετανοέω deals with the source of our motives, not with conduct, or even with the motives themselves. In fact, Campbell recognized the danger of this.[37]

John Calvin and George Campbell were primarily interested in the theological and religious significance of this problem. Let us now turn to a group of men who sought to divest themselves of theological or religious presuppositions as they looked at the words μετανοέω and μετάνοια. De Quincey, famed for his mastery of all things Greek, confessed, in conversation with Lady Carbury, that he had "always been irritated by the entire irrelevance of the English word 'repentance' and by something very like cant, on which the whole burden of the passage ["Repent ye: for the kingdom of heaven is at hand"] had been thrown. How was it any natural preparation for a vast spiritual revolution that men should, first of all, acknowledge any special duty of *repentance?* The *repentance*, if any movement of that nature could be intelligently supposed called for, should more naturally follow this great revolution — which as yet, both in its principle and its purpose, was altogether mysterious — than herald it or ground it. *In my opinion the Greek 'μετάνοια' concealed a most profound meaning — a meaning of prodigious compass — which bore no allusion to any ideas whatsoever of repentance.* The μετά carried with it an emphatic expression of its original idea — the idea of transfer, of translation; or, if we prefer a Grecian to a Roman apparelling, the idea of *metamorphosis*. And this idea, to what is it applied? Upon what object is the idea of spiritual transfiguration made to bear? Simply on the noetic or intellectual faculty — the faculty of shaping and conceiving things under their true relations." [38]

De Quincey applied this perception of things under

The Need for a Restudy

new relations to moral truth, to the nature of the new and spiritual revelation which is to be given. Men's minds must be transfigured to comprehend the new revelation which is to come through Christ, the Finisher of prophecy (Heb. 1:1-3), the perfect Revealer (John 14:9; 1:18). The Apostle Paul is a perfect example of the need of a transfigured mind in order to understand Jesus, and of the results from such transfiguration.

Coleridge and Matthew Arnold, both, felt keen dissatisfaction with " repent " and " repentance " as translations of these Greek words. Coleridge [39] suggested " transmentation " to describe the mental transfiguration which both John and Jesus called for: a transposed mind which thinks new thoughts, aspires for better things and acknowledges a new sovereignty — God's will, not one's own.

Matthew Arnold defined repentance as follows: " To have the *thoughts in order* as to certain matters of *conduct.* This was the ' method ' of Jesus: *setting up a great unceasing inward movement of attention and verification in matters which are three-fourths of human life (righteousness) where to see true and to verify is not difficult.* . . . Watch carefully what passes *within you,* that you may obey the voice of conscience. . . . This, we say, is the method of Jesus. To it belongs his use of that important word which in the

Greek is 'metanoia.' We translate it 'repentance,' a mourning and lamenting over our sins; and we translate it wrong. Of 'metanoia,' as Jesus used the word, the lamenting one's sins was a small part; the main part was something far more active and fruitful, *the setting up of an immense new inward movement for obtaining the rule of life.* And 'metanoia,' accordingly, is a change of the inner man." [40]

It was hoped that when the revisers of the Authorized Version did their work,[41] they would take note of the inadequate translation of John's and Jesus' challenge, "Repent ye; for the kingdom of heaven is at hand." But, for reasons sufficient to them, they did not change the familiar words. In this they were followed by the American scholars who produced the Revised Version twenty years later.

Treadwell Walden,[42] in a searching and illuminating discussion, lamented this failure. The assumption of the revisers seemed to be that, while "repentance" was not originally an adequate rendering of *metanoia*, in the thought of the Church the word "repentance" had become established and had taken on the fuller meaning it should have. But this is just what the word has not done, even in the minds of the clergy as a whole, and how much less in the minds of the laity! It is disappointing to see that such excellent modern translations as Weymouth's, Moffatt's, and Good-

The Need for a Restudy 45

speed's do not give us any more light here. They follow the crowd with, "Repent ye."

The modern German translation of the New Testament by Ludwig Albrecht [43] has caught the meaning of Jesus admirably: "*Ändert euern Sinn*," i.e., "Change (alter) your mind." It should be noted that the German word *Sinn* is somewhat broader than the English word "mind," for it includes the "tastes" and "inclinations." It is the tastes and inclinations of men that must be changed, before the conduct of men improves. This position is strongly supported by Moulton and Milligan,[44] who show from the papyri that repentance calls for "a complete change of attitude, spiritual and moral, toward God."

It is out of a great conviction that the quality of Western Christendom has seriously suffered that I felt it worth while to re-examine this whole matter. Scholars have known the correct meaning of "repentance" for centuries. It is now time for the pastor to tell his people. This must be done, if popular Christianity is to be put on the right foundation.

In Jesus' day, religious routine occupied the mind and the time of men. When that was performed, the interest in religion was exhausted. The gaze was turned to the past. Religious minutiae were more important than humanity. The "pious" trusted in themselves that they were righteous and set all others at nought. It was this interpretation of religion that lay back of Jesus' words, "For I say unto you, that except your righteousness shall exceed the righteousness of the scribes and Pharisees, ye shall in no wise enter into the kingdom of heaven" (Matt. 5:20).

It was an essentially wrong idea of religion that disqualified the Pharisee for entering the Kingdom. This is suggested in Jesus' conversation with Nicodemus: "Verily, verily, I say unto thee, Except one be born anew, he cannot see the kingdom of God" (John 3:3). Regeneration is necessary before one comprehends the Kingdom of God, and it is therefore necessary before one can enter it: "Except one be born of water and the Spirit, he cannot enter into the kingdom of God" (John 3:5). The Gospel of John does not use the words "repent" or "repentance"; but we have the equivalent here: regeneration. Matthew reports Jesus as saying to his disciples, "Except ye turn, and become as little children, ye shall in no wise enter into the kingdom of heaven" (Matt. 18:3). These words seem to equate "conversion," "turning," with rebirth. Both the words to Nicodemus and the words to the disciples state that a mental transfiguration is necessary for participating in the Kingdom. A childlike receptivity to new ideas is an absolute essential to understanding the Kingdom and, therefore, to entering it. This throws light, then, on the reason Jesus gives for "repentance": "For the kingdom of heaven is at hand" — God was opening the doors of opportunity to men. To enjoy it, they must undergo a mental transfiguration, which we call "repentance." Repentance looks ahead in hope and anticipation; regret, remorse, looks backward in shame and forward in fear.

Able scholars have long been protesting against the inadequate meaning given to μετάνοια, but their voices have been lonely cries in the wilderness of preconceived ideas. The mass of Christendom has passed by unheeding, continuing to think of repentance in terms of regret, sorrow, introspection, and man-made satisfaction for sin, instead of a transformation of mind in preparation for fellowship in the Kingdom of God.

Repentance is a pilgrimage from the mind of the flesh to the mind of Christ. The mind of Christ is necessary to full fellowship with Christ.

And they went out, and preached that men should repent. — Mark 6:12.

2

THE NEW TESTAMENT EMPHASIS ON REPENTANCE

It is human for our minds to return frequently to those things that we regard as of supreme importance. By this criterion, " repentance " stands in the forefront of the important doctrines of the New Testament. We shall examine, in detail, the words of John the Baptist, Jesus, and the apostles.

John the Baptist's Preaching

As we have said, the opening note of the New Testament, " Repent ye; for the kingdom of heaven is at hand " (Matt. 3:2), reverberates throughout the entire New Testament. These words of the Forerunner are preparatory to the coming of the King, the Messiah. As Matthew relates them, they are designed to make ready the way of the Lord (Matt. 3:3). As the Gospel of John pictures the work of the Baptist, he " came for witness, that he might bear witness of the light, that all might believe through him " (John 1:7). Putting the words of Matthew and John together, it would seem that the Forerunner's task was to pave the way for men to understand and accept the teachings and claims of Christ.

What the Baptist meant by "repentance" is indicated in his words: "Bring forth therefore fruit worthy of repentance: and think not to say within yourselves, We have Abraham to our father: for I say unto you, that God is able of these stones to raise up children unto Abraham. And even now the axe lieth at the root of the trees: every tree therefore that bringeth not forth good fruit is hewn down, and cast into the fire" (Matt. 3:8–10). Repentance is to have a twofold issue: reformation in conduct, and transformation of mental outlook. John demanded conduct worthy of men who have reoriented themselves in their relations to God. Instead of finding a sense of security in their racial privileges, as the seed of Abraham, they must face the fact, that, in the Messianic age, each man shall stand or fall by his personal relationship to God.

Racial heritage can no longer be used as a cloak for evil living. Fruit-bearing is the "acid test" of acceptability. The ax of God's judgment is ready to hew down every tree that brings not forth good fruit. These words paved the way for such teaching of Jesus as, e.g., that embedded in the parable of the Barren Fig Tree (Luke 13:6–9). A nonproductive tree must not be allowed to cumber the ground in the vineyard. The fruitless branches must not be left to drain the vine of its vitality. Productivity is the price of survival in the Kingdom.

According to Luke's account (Luke 3:10, 11) when the multitudes asked, "What then must we do?" John replied, "He that hath two coats, let him impart to him that hath none; and he that hath food, let him do likewise." This is preparatory for such teachings as that in the story of the Rich Man and Lazarus (Luke 16:19–31): calloused indulgence in the delicacies of life, coupled with indifference to the destitution of one's fellow man, even though he be a sore-ridden beggar, excludes one from the Kingdom and brings down God's judgment, unremitting and unrelieved.

To the publicans who, accepting John's baptism (Luke 3:12, 13), came asking, "Teacher, what must we do," he replied, "Extort no more than that which is appointed you." In like manner, to the soldiers, John replied, "Extort from no man by violence, neither accuse any one wrongfully; and be content with your wages" (Luke 3:14). The multitudes, the publicans, and the soldiers sensed that John's challenge, "Repent ye; for the kingdom of heaven is at hand," called for a reformation of life. He had announced the coming of the Kingdom and the consequent necessity of a "change of mind," a metamorphosis in their thinking; it was no longer sufficient to be descended from Abraham. These groups felt that they must " do " something about it. It is true that, when John made specific recommendations, he dealt with actions rather than with motives and thought processes. We shall see in the next chapter how Jesus carried the idea of repentance into the realm of men's aspirations, ideals, and standards of value.

It is provocative of thought that Luke did not represent the scribes, the Pharisees, or the priests, as making any inquiry as to what they should do. Was that prophetic of the fact that, as a whole, they had no intention of changing their ideals; that to the end they opposed Jesus' concept of righteousness, of the Kingdom; and that finally they hounded him to the cross?

Jesus' Preaching

When Jesus began his ministry, he accepted the message of John as the core of his own (Matt. 4:17); enlarging, enriching and ennobling John's conception of repentance. His greatest emphasis lay in correcting men's thinking on the basic things of life: happiness, righteousness, the nature of God and of his Kingdom.

The first recorded teaching of Jesus, following his opening message, "Repent ye; for the kingdom of heaven is at hand," is the Sermon on the Mount. This is an admirable example of how Jesus sought to change men's preconceptions by offering a new set of ideas, a new standard of values. In fact, so different was this standard from that in common acceptance, that he had to take precautions against being regarded as a revolutionary, whose work would undermine "the faith of the fathers." "Think not," he said, "that I came to destroy the law or the prophets: I came not to destroy, but to fulfil" (Matt. 5:17). In other words, Jesus was calling men to a real understanding of the faith of the fathers.

Isaiah had stated the need for repentance in its profounder sense, and the consequence of the absence of such repentance, when he said, "For my thoughts are not your thoughts, neither are your ways my ways, saith Jehovah" (Isa. 55:8). When men's thoughts cease to resemble God's thoughts, their conduct ceases to be godly. This, in a nutshell, is the importance of the New Testament doctrine of repentance: it is a calling of men's minds to be patterned after God's, in order that their conduct may be in keeping with his will and that they may participate in his reign. This divergence of thought, with its consequences and its cure, is the burden of the New Testament message. The New Testament writers do not allow the readers' minds to wander long from this idea. Repeatedly and insistently, we are brought back to face the demand, "Change your mind," transfigure your ideals, transpose your set of values.

Jesus' Instructions

When Jesus sent forth the Twelve, "they went out, and preached that men should repent" (Mark 6:12). It was not enough, apparently, to cast out demons and to heal the sick; it was necessary to change men's thinking, to transfigure their aspirations and their ambitions. The Church has forgotten this, to its own confusion and frustration. Introspective agonizing over sin does very little good, if the old desires and ambitions which led the Christian into sin are left unchanged. Afflicting the soul and torturing the body do not remove the cause of the sins which men punish in themselves. When the Twelve preached repentance, they were attacking the origin of sin. They called for a change in the life design of men. As changes in the architect's blueprint bring changes in the house that is constructed, so changes in a man's life design result in changes in his character. If the Church had insisted throughout its history on the importance of the Christian's pattern for living, the pattern of Christian ethics would not present the crazy-quilt effect that it does today.

When Jesus sent forth the Seventy, their work also

was to issue in repentance. The one ground of condemnation for Chorazin, Bethsaida, and Capernaum was that they did not "repent." With the same opportunity, Tyre and Sidon "would have repented long ago, sitting in sackcloth and ashes" (Luke 10:13). "The men of Nineveh shall stand up in the judgment with this generation, and shall condemn it: for they repented at the preaching of Jonah; and behold, a greater than Jonah is here" (Luke 11:32). The Seventy, like the Twelve, went forth primarily to call men to "repentance."

It is confusing, to the popular mind, to turn to The Book of Jonah [45] and discover that it does not say that the men of Nineveh repented. Thrice, "repent" is used of God, but not once of man. Upon what grounds does the Lord say that the men of Nineveh "repented" at the preaching of Jonah? There was a drastic reformation in their conduct. The city, notorious for its wickedness, is confronted with the words of the prophet: "Yet forty days, and Nineveh shall be overthrown." We are told that "the people of Nineveh believed God; and they proclaimed a fast, and put on sackcloth, from the greatest of them even to the least of them. And the tidings reached the king of Nineveh, and he arose from his throne, and laid his robe from him, and covered him with sackcloth, and sat in ashes. And he made proclamation and published through Nineveh by the decree of the king and his nobles, saying, Let neither man nor beast, herd nor flock, taste anything; let them not feed, nor drink water; but let them be covered with sackcloth, both man and beast, and let them cry mightily unto God: yea, let them turn every one from his evil way, and from the violence that is in his hands. Who knoweth whether God will not turn and repent, and turn away from his fierce anger, that we perish not? And God saw their works, that they turned from their evil way; and God repented of the evil which he said he would do unto them; and he did it not " (Jonah 3:4b–10).

Undoubtedly, fear played a very real part in Nineveh's repentance, but it was also accompanied by a real reformation of conduct: a *turning from evil ways and the violence in their hands.* This was based on a newly acquired belief in God. Little is said about a basic change in life viewpoint, but it is implied, even though of a temporary nature. It should, however, be kept in mind that Ninevite repentance should hardly be expected to be on as high a plane as Christian repentance.

Not only did Jesus send forth his disciples to preach repentance, but he stated that the purpose of his own ministry was to call men to repentance: "I am not come to call the righteous but sinners to repentance" (Luke 5:32).[46] In John 10:10, Jesus is represented as saying that he came that men might have life and have it more abundantly. These two statements are essentially one. A change of mind from the selfish human outlook to the self-giving mind of Christ leads to abundant living. As Jesus put it, "Whosoever would save his life shall lose it; and whosoever shall lose his life for my sake and the gospel's shall save it" (Mark 8:35). Self-seeking is self-destructive; self-giving results in self-discovery. Dr. John McDowell has said, "In religion as in astronomy everything depends on what you make the center." Ptolemaic astronomy made the earth the center of the universe; consequently all its conclusions were wrong. Unregenerate man makes his own desires and aspirations the center of his spiritual universe; so his conclusions are often just the opposite of those of the man who makes God the center of his aspirations. The pagan tries to bring God in line with his plans; the Christian says, "Not my will, but thine, be done." Christian repentance includes the discovery of this new center for life, the adopting of a new regulatory principle — the will of God, not the appetites of self.

God's Eternal Purpose

At the end of the journey to Emmaus, after Jesus had "opened" the minds of the two disconsolate disciples "that they might understand the scriptures," he said, "Thus it is written, that the Christ should suffer, and rise again from the dead the third day; and that repentance and remission of sins should be preached in his name unto all the nations, beginning from Jerusalem" (Luke 24:46, 47). Thus it appears that the "repentance" of all mankind and the consequent removal of their sins were embedded in the eternal counsel of God, just as definitely as the Crucifixion and the Resurrection. In fact, the Crucifixion and the Resurrection were preparatory to "repentance."

The Christ, who emptied himself rather than assert himself, demonstrated in his own ministry what God expects of his people. Before redemption can be completed, a man must be brought to see this. We think too much of redemption in terms of rescue from hell. It is primarily rescue from one's self. As the Pioneer and Perfecter of *the* faith, i.e., Christian faith, Jesus not only showed the *way*, but he brought faith to its maturity: he demonstrated the power of faith at its best. A world dominated by men of such faith would be something very close to the Kingdom of God; a world dominated by the slogan, "Every man for himself and the Devil take the hindmost," is a world after the Devil's own heart. "Repentance," in the New Testament sense, involves a change from the philosophy of the Devil to that of Christ, " who for the joy that was set before him endured the cross, despising shame," to redeem men from the philosophy of the Devil. The Church has not brought this fact home to the people forcefully.

The Apostles' Preaching

The book of The Acts records how God's purpose of preaching repentance to all nations was carried out. All apostolic preaching emphasized the necessity of repentance. Stephen's sermon is no exception. Although he did not use the word repent, he clearly called for the act: " Ye stiffnecked and uncircumcised in heart and ears, ye do always resist the Holy Spirit: as your fathers did, so do ye. Which of the prophets did not your fathers persecute? and they killed them that showed before of the coming of the Righteous One; of whom ye have now become betrayers and murderers; ye who received the law as it was ordained by angels, and kept it not " (Acts 7: 51–53). Throughout its history Israel had striven against God's purpose, and even now fought bitterly against God, said Stephen.

Next to the Resurrection, " repentance " is the most frequent theme in The Acts. In every situation but two, the Resurrection is directly linked to the preaching of repentance as the ground of the appeal. The first exception is in Peter's words to Simon Magus:

"Repent therefore of this thy wickedness, and pray the Lord, if perhaps the thought of thy heart shall be forgiven thee" (Acts 8:22). Simon had heard about the Resurrection from Philip. His needs were of another sort: a new heart, not a new hope. The second exception is Paul's farewell address to the Ephesian elders at Miletus (Acts 20:18-35). They were seasoned Christians, familiar with the fundamental teachings of the apostles. Paul was simply taking final leave of them. It was not necessary to take up the matter of the Resurrection.

Peter's Emphasis

Repentance was Peter's message on every important occasion: on Pentecost (Acts 2:38), to the crowd in Solomon's porch (Acts 3:19), before the Sanhedrin (Acts 5:31), and to Simon Magus (Acts 8:22). In the case of Cornelius, we are not told that Peter preached repentance, but we are told that the household did repent (Acts 11:18).

It is worth noting that Peter always uses the verb "repent" in the imperative mode and in the aorist tense. The imperative mode is normal for this verb in the New Testament, but the aorist imperative is characteristic of Peter and of the Apocalypse. Each was dealing with an urgent situation. Peter was calling for immediate decision on the question of the Messiahship of Jesus. His own people had regarded Him as an impostor, a false prophet, who richly deserved his fate; but God approved him, as was evidenced in the mighty works, the signs and the wonders, which God did through him; and God had raised him up and made him both Lord and Christ. This Jesus, whom they had despised and rejected, Peter asked them to accept as their true Messiah and to submit to him as their Lord and King.

Repentance, here, calls for far more than contrition, sorrow for sin. They were " pricked in their heart," but they recognized that that was not enough. So they cried out, " Brethren, what shall we do? " Peter called for a reversal of their judgment of Jesus: " Repent ye, and be baptized every one of you in the name of Jesus Christ unto the remission of your sins; and ye shall receive the gift of the Holy Spirit " (Acts 2:38). Since they were so completely out of line with God, there was only one thing to do; they must reverse themselves completely. Jesus, the Nazarene, the supposed impostor, was really Jesus, the Christ. Repentance included the recognition of this as a fact of prime importance.

Again, after the healing of the lame man at the Beautiful Gate of the Temple, Peter denied that any virtue lay in him or John to heal the man, but " the

God of Abraham, and of Isaac, and of Jacob, the God of our fathers, hath glorified his Servant Jesus; whom ye delivered up, and denied before the face of Pilate, when he had determined to release him. But ye denied the Holy and Righteous One, and asked for a murderer to be granted unto you, and killed the Prince of life; whom God raised from the dead; whereof we are witnesses. And by faith in his name hath his name made this man strong, whom ye behold and know: yea, the faith which is through him hath given him this perfect soundness in the presence of you all" (Acts 3:13–16). Peter contrasted their attitude toward Jesus with that of God in a manner devastating to their self-respect: "God glorified him; ye denied him. Ye killed him; God raised him up. Ye chose Barabbas, a murderer, as your ideal, and caused the Author of life to be killed. This lame man who stands before you healed is a living testimony that Jesus is the Author of life. Even Pilate, the hated profligate, wanted to let Jesus go, but you howled him down." This kind of preaching was not calculated to make the congregation comfortable. The climax of this sermon was a call for repentance: "Repent ye therefore, and turn again, that your sins may be blotted out, that so there may come seasons of refreshing from the presence of the Lord; and that he may send the Christ who hath been appointed for you, even Jesus: whom the heaven must receive until the times of restoration of all things, whereof God spake by the mouth of his holy prophets that have been from of old" (Acts 3:19–21).

Reversal of mind toward this Jesus was necessary: "He is God's appointed Messiah. Your sins cannot be blotted out and seasons of refreshing cannot come to you until you receive him. You are out of line with God's plans and out of step with the prophets. Repentance, reversal of mind, is a prerequisite to sharing in God's reign. Seasons of refreshing come only to those who accept Jesus at God's evaluation," said Peter. The aorist tense of the verb repent pointed to the urgency of this decision.

John and Jesus called for a repentance that covered all of life as a preparation for the Kingdom; Peter called, with the one exception, Simon Magus, for a change of mind on one point: the Messiahship of Jesus — the right of Jesus to call for "repentance." "Him did God exalt with his right hand to be a Prince and a Saviour, to give repentance to Israel, and remission of sins" (Acts 5:31). Everywhere Peter emphasized the necessity of reversal of mind before blessing can come.

Paul's Emphasis

According to Paul, his own ministry was initiated and characterized by preaching repentance: "Wherefore, O king Agrippa, I was not disobedient unto the heavenly vision: but declared both to them of Damascus first, and at Jerusalem, and throughout all the country of Judæa, and also to the Gentiles, that they should repent and turn to God, doing works worthy of repentance" (Acts 26:19, 20).

According to the account of Paul's conversion in Acts, ch. 9, he preached that Jesus "is the Son of God" (Acts 9:20), "proving that this is the Christ" (Acts 9:22). The preaching of repentance and the preaching that Jesus "is the Son of God," the Christ, were, for Paul, inseparable if not identical themes. For one who, a few days before, was "breathing threatening and slaughter against the disciples of the Lord" (Acts 9:1) to contend mightily with the Jews that He is their Messiah, the Son of God, represents just the sort of mental revolution involved in the New Testament idea of repentance. The man who fumed at Christ and hated and hounded his followers later could say, "For to me to live is Christ" (Phil. 1:21). Paul referred to this change of viewpoint: "Wherefore we henceforth know no man after the flesh: even though we have known Christ after the flesh, yet now we

The New Testament Emphasis

know him so no more" (II Cor. 5:16). After Damascus, he ceased to judge either men or Christ by fleshly standards, although, formerly, he had done just that. Being in Christ had made him a new creature with new standards of value; all things, including Christ and mankind, had taken on a new aspect for him. This is essential to repentance.

Of those who occupied his old position with regard to Christ, Paul could say: "I say the truth in Christ, I lie not, my conscience bearing witness with me in the Holy Spirit, that I have great sorrow and unceasing pain in my heart. For I could wish that I myself were anathema from Christ for my brethren's sake, my kinsmen according to the flesh" (Rom. 9:1–3). This was a far cry from the man who could persecute and kill all who differed with him in religion.

Before Paul's conversion he could not have conceded that there were any redeeming features about those who differed from him in theological views, but now he is a different man; he has experienced a reversal of mind about Christ which has reversed his character. "If any man is in Christ, he is a new creature: the old things are passed away; behold, they are become new" (II Cor. 5:17), is an autobiographical statement. To repeat, Paul is the greatest example in Christian history of what repentance does to a man.

Paul launched his mission to the Gentiles at Antioch

of Pisidia, preaching Christ as a crucified, risen Saviour, basing his message on John's preaching of repentance (Acts 13:24, 30). At Athens, Paul told his audience: "The times of ignorance therefore God overlooked; but now he commandeth men that they should all everywhere repent" (Acts 17:30). Repentance, for the Athenians, meant, in part, changing their ideas about God: "Being then the offspring of God, we ought not to think that the Godhead is like unto gold, or silver, or stone, graven by art and device of man" (Acts 17:29). God, according to Paul, is a universal Personality in whom men live and move and have their being. Repentance requires men to leave their idolatries behind, to press on to know the infinite, eternal, creative God.

Repentance, according to Paul, presupposed new revelation: as God made a new disclosure of himself in Christ, he called for a change of mind on moral, ethical, and religious issues. This is what makes the Christian era pre-eminently and emphatically an era when repentance is demanded. Men must think of God in new terms, and treat their fellow men in a new way. Jeremy Taylor acutely observed, "That the Gospel is a covenant of repentance, is evident in the whole design and nature of the thing, in the preparatory sermons made by the Baptist, by the apostles of our Lord, by the seventy-two disciples, and the ex-

The New Testament Emphasis

hortations made by St. Peter at the first opening of the commission and is the secret of the religion. Which doctrine of repentance, lest it be thought to be a permission to sin, a leave to need the remedy, is charged with an addition of a strict and severe holiness, the precept of perfection. It therefore must be such a repentance as includes in it perfection, and yet the perfection is such as needs repentance." [47]

In saying that repentance " includes in it perfection and yet the perfection is such as needs repentance," did Bishop Taylor mean that it must be a genuine, an actual, change of mind, and yet that to be genuine repentance must be progressive? This is in line with the present imperative in Jesus' words and also with Calvin's statement that repentance is lifelong. The pilgrimage from the mind of the flesh to the mind of Christ is never quite complete while we are in the flesh, but the pilgrim must be advancing.

As Paul made his last journey back to Jerusalem, he gathered about him the Ephesian elders for a farewell. As he reviewed his ministry among them, he reminded them that it had been a ministry of preaching repentance toward God, both to Greeks and Jews, and faith toward Christ (Acts 20:21). This had been accomplished with tears and trials, plots and riots. The plots and riots grew out of a clash of viewpoints; the tears and trials resulted because Ephesus did not wish to reverse all the values of cultured paganism and accept a God on the cross, instead of great Diana. Paul's soul and body served as buffer between the clashing viewpoints.

In Paul's final recorded public utterance, he reminded Agrippa that his ministry had been one of preaching repentance from the Damascus road (Acts 26:20) to the judgment seat, and that it was this message which prompted the Jews to attempt to kill him (Acts 26:21).

The Epistles of Paul

When we pass out of the book of The Acts to the Pauline epistles, it is surprising to find the words repent and repentance used so seldom. The verb occurs only once (II Cor. 12:21); and the noun, four times. The most striking of these passages is: " Or despisest thou the riches of his goodness and forbearance and longsuffering, not knowing that the goodness of God leadeth thee to repentance?" (Rom. 2:4.)

What has happened? Has Paul, the missionary, ceased to preach and write about repentance? Has the reporting of Paul's ministry in The Acts been colored by Luke? The answer seems to be," No! " Paul was writing to Christians. They had heard his message of repentance and remission of sins. He did not

The New Testament Emphasis

need to rehearse the A B C's for them. As an illustration of how completely silent Paul could be on one of his great themes, it is well to recall that, although Paul mentions the Law seventy-two times in the Epistle to the Romans, he never mentions it once in II Corinthians, an epistle of comparable length.

In his letters, Paul was still inculcating the Christian conception of repentance, but he was using different words. To the Philippians he said, "Have this mind in you, which was also in Christ Jesus" (Phil. 2:5). To the Romans he said, "For the mind of the flesh is death; but the mind of the Spirit is life and peace: because the mind of the flesh is enmity against God; for it is not subject to the law of God, neither indeed can it be: and they that are in the flesh cannot please God" (Rom. 8:6–8). To the Corinthians he wrote, "God was in Christ reconciling the world unto himself, not reckoning unto them their trespasses, and having committed unto us the word of reconciliation" (II Cor. 5:19). Repentance is essentially "not looking each of you to his own things, but each of you also to the things of others" (Phil. 2:4): having the mind of Christ. It is passing from the mind of the flesh to the mind of the spirit. It is reconciliation with God on the basis of his infinite grace in Christ Jesus.

Here we have the nub of the matter. A good and gracious God has provided a way to bring a rebellious, sinning world into harmony with himself. This he does by not counting the sins of men against them. This is the goodness of God leading men to repentance, a change of mind toward God, from the mind of the flesh with its hostility, to the mind of Christ with its spirit of self-emptying love — even to the death on the cross. From the spirit of self-assertion man moves toward a spirit which says, "Not my will, but thine, be done." This is reconciliation, according to Paul (II Cor. 5: 18–20); this is repentance in its fullest sense. There will be sorrow for sin and there will be reform of conduct, but neither of these is an equivalent to or a substitute for repentance. Repentance involves a migration from the mind of the flesh to the mind of Christ.

The Epistle to the Hebrews

There are only three references to repentance in Hebrews, but the whole effort of the author was to change the thinking of a group of Christians who were tending to revert to Judaism. Apparently they feared that they had deserted the faith of the fathers; the author sought to convince them of the utter superiority of Christianity, of the necessity of advancing to maturity of faith in God and fellowship with him: " Wherefore leaving the doctrine of the first principles

The New Testament Emphasis

of Christ, let us press on unto perfection; not laying again a foundation of repentance from dead works, and of faith toward God, of the teaching of baptisms, and of laying on of hands, and of resurrection of the dead, and of eternal judgment. And this will we do, if God permit" (Heb. 6:1–3). The "perfection" to which the writer wished to press on was an adequate understanding of the absolutely efficacious priesthood of Christ, who is "able to save to the uttermost" those who come to God through him.

But the writer follows this exhortation with a very solemn warning of the impossibility of renewing again "unto repentance" those who were once enlightened and have tasted the heavenly gift, have been made partakers of the Holy Spirit, and have tasted the good word of God and the powers of the age to come, and then fall away again. The reason is that they "crucify up" for themselves the Son of God, exposing him to public ridicule. This passage illustrates the profounder meaning of repentance. Men, like Judas, may say repeatedly, "I have sinned." But a sense of guilt is not the equivalent of repentance. When a man has come up to the rather full Christian experience outlined above, and then reverses himself for his own advantage and betrays his Saviour, something has gone out of him that cannot be restored. If repentance is no more than an accusing conscience, there may be repeated cycles of sin and self-accusation. But if repentance is a reversal of a man's whole moral nature, his whole mental outlook, he cannot continue reversing himself. It should be said again here that repentance is never complete, but it must keep progressing in one general direction toward the mind of Christ.

The General Epistles

There is one reference in II Peter: "The Lord is not slack concerning his promise, as some count slackness; but is longsuffering to you-ward, not wishing that any should perish, but that all should come to repentance" (II Peter 3:9). If II Peter is from the middle of the second century, as some scholars believe, we still have the Christian conviction that it is God's purpose to lead all men to the change of mind and heart which brings them in harmony with himself. "Longsuffering" is God's means to lead men to repentance, to reconciliation, to the transition from the mind of the flesh to the mind of Christ.

While neither "repent" nor "repentance" occurs in I Peter, the idea is prominent. This is evidenced especially in the new attitude toward suffering. This epistle is really an excellent commentary on the Beatitude, "Blessed are they that have been persecuted for righteousness' sake: for theirs is the kingdom of

The New Testament Emphasis

heaven" (Matt. 5:10). It represents the "new mind" toward suffering. Suffering is not any longer to be regarded as a direct judgment from God for specific sins. The Book of Job had anticipated the Christian answer; Jesus gave it. The eighteen men upon whom the tower of Siloam fell were not necessarily "offenders above all the men that dwell in Jerusalem" (Luke 13:4). The man born blind (John 9:1–3) was not necessarily a great sinner, nor were his parents: God was manifesting his works of redemption and healing in him. That there is a redemptive, beneficent purpose running through the sufferings of the righteous, Peter argued with great force: "But even if ye should suffer for righteousness' sake, blessed are ye: and fear not their fear, neither be troubled" (I Peter 3:14). Repentance includes this new philosophy of suffering.

No word for "repent" or "repentance" occurs in The Epistle of James, but, even more widely than I Peter, James offered a new philosophy of life. The testing of a Christian is to be received with joy, not groaning (James 1:2–12); the profession of the Christian faith is not a substitute for Christian conduct (James 1:19–27); neither poverty nor riches should affect a man's standing in the Christian society (James 2:1–9); partial obedience is disobedience, not a satisfactory substitute for obedience (James 2:10–13); inactive faith is not faith (James 2:14–26); half loyalty to God is disloyalty (James 4:4–10). James left no place for a smug religion; neither does repentance.

The Epistles of John, like the Gospel, do not use either "repent" or "repentance," but they are shot through and through with the idea. A clear distinction is made between righteousness and "piosity," sanctimonious professions: "He that saith, I know him, and keepeth not his commandments, is a liar, and the truth is not in him" (I John 2:4); "if we say that we have fellowship with him and walk in the darkness, we lie, and do not the truth" (I John 1:6); "he that saith he is in the light and hateth his brother, is in the darkness even until now" (I John 2:9); "he that doeth righteousness is righteous" (I John 3:7) — not he that talks righteously. For some professing Christians these demands represent a mental transfiguration.

The origin and nature of Christian love also comes in for discussion: "Herein is love, not that we loved God, but that he loved us, and sent his Son to be the propitiation for our sins" (I John 4:10); "we love, because he first loved us. If a man say, I love God, and hateth his brother, he is a liar: for he that loveth not his brother whom he hath seen, cannot love God whom he hath not seen" (I John 4:19, 20).

Last, but basic to all, is the attitude toward Christ: "Who is the liar but he that denieth that Jesus is the Christ? This is the antichrist, even he that denieth the

The New Testament Emphasis

Father and the Son " (I John 2:22). This statement, like others along the same line, was aimed at Cerinthian Gnosticism, which degraded Christ. To degrade Jesus is to dishonor God; to exalt Christ is to glorify God. Repentance involved a reversal of the Gnostic judgment as to the nature of righteousness, of love, and of Christ.

The most important thing, however, for our study, in I John, is how this change in mind is brought about: " Ye know that every one also that doeth righteousness is begotten of him " (I John 2:29); " whosoever is begotten of God doeth no sin, because his seed abideth in him: and he cannot sin, because he is begotten of God " (I John 3:9). It is clear from I John that the transformed view of all things, which we call " repentance," is bound up with regeneration — being begotten of God. This should be associated with Jesus' words to Nicodemus: Except ye be born again ye can neither comprehend nor enter the Kingdom. This will be discussed further in Chapter V.

The Apocalypse

When we pass to the Apocalypse, we find much said about " repentance " — eleven instances — and it is always the verb that is used. Seven of these instances were addressed to Christians who had fallen away from the freshness of their faith. They are all in the aorist imperative, implying great urgency in the appeal. The Church was losing the freshness of its vision. The mind of Christ was no longer the mind of the Church.

The church at Ephesus had toiled and endured; it had not tolerated wicked men; it had tested the false prophets and discovered that they were liars: it had borne its burdens for the name of Christ and not grown weary: but it had lost the freshness of its first love. Repentance for its cooling love was its only hope: "Remember therefore whence thou art fallen, and repent and do the first works; or else I come to thee, and will move thy candlestick out of its place, except thou repent" (Rev. 2:5). The lesson is: God takes the light away from a loveless mind.

The church at Pergamum, although it dwelt where Satan's throne was, had not denied Christ's name. It had been true even to martyrdom. Its outstanding weakness was that it clung to the teachings of Balaam, who taught Balak to put a stumbling block in the way of the people: Unless they repent, Christ will draw the two-edged sword of his mouth (Rev. 2:16). From the loveless God withdraws the light; against the corrupt he draws a sword, the truth.

The church at Thyatira had works, love, faith. It had rendered service and persevered under trial, but it tolerated a false prophetess. It had been given time to repent, but did not wish to do so. Those who shared its evil-doing were destined for the great tribulation, unless they repented (Rev. 2:21, 22).

Of the church at Laodicea nothing good is said. It was neither hot nor cold and, therefore, disgusting to God. It boasted of its riches and self-sufficiency, but, in reality, it was pitiable, poor, naked, and blind. "I counsel thee," said the Lord, "to buy of me gold refined by fire, that thou mayest become rich; and white garments, that thou mayest clothe thyself, and that the shame of thy nakedness be not made manifest; and eyesalve to anoint thine eyes, that thou mayest see. As many as I love, I reprove and chasten: be zealous therefore, and repent" (Rev. 3:18, 19). A lukewarm church is told to be zealous, to boil; to reverse itself — to change its mind from cold self-sufficiency to zealous loyalty.

It is challenging to note that that most gracious invitation: "Behold, I stand at the door and knock: if any man hear my voice and open the door, I will come in to him, and will sup with him, and he with me" (Rev. 3:20), was addressed to this lukewarm, self-satisfied church. God goes to the utmost limit to redeem even a disgusting church. To the Apocalyptist, as to Paul, it is the goodness of God that leads to repentance.

Conclusion

The important fact for our purpose is that the first note and the last note struck in the New Testament is repentance. It is the most universal note in the New Testament, even more so than the Resurrection. This is especially noteworthy in light of the fact that it was belief in the Resurrection that made Christian preaching possible. Repentance gave Christian preaching its objective.

We shall now examine the New Testament for the implications of this idea which is stressed so constantly.

For I say unto you, that except your righteousness shall exceed the righteousness of the scribes and Pharisees, ye shall in no wise enter into the kingdom of heaven. — Matt. 5:20.

3

THE IMPLICATIONS OF REPENTANCE

We face a new day in our world; the old ways can never be restored. This is not a cause for unmitigated regret. We should rather thank God and take courage, for we believe that God is working through history. The constant demand for repentance throughout the New Testament cannot be disregarded by the Christian.

Our most urgent need is to discover God's will for our participation in this new day. It is this fact that makes the implications of repentance so important, for they impinge upon every phase of life and thought. We must reverse our minds where they are not Christian. The message, " Repent ye," is as valid today as when it first came from the lips of John and Jesus, and it is as urgently needed as then. We need to repent, in the New Testament sense, in order to understand and participate in the Kingdom as God establishes it. Zeal for God without knowledge is always tragic.

God

Many of Jesus' parables were directed at the Pharisaic misunderstanding of God. The Church has not been free from misunderstanding God and misrepresenting him. Christian civilization has said, "Lord, Lord," but built its house on the sands of hearing and not doing. We have seen our house collapse. We must rebuild the hard way by digging down to the bedrock of right thinking about God, followed by a right response to God, for everything hinges on these two.

A primary emphasis in the New Testament is that God has a purpose for his world; existence does not move through a meaningless series of cycles without end. This long-range purpose roots in the promise to Abraham: "I will bless thee, . . . and in thee shall all the families of the earth be blessed" (Gen. 12:2, 3). In the fullness of the time "God sent forth his Son" that men might have the life abundant.

God, according to the New Testament, is carrying through this purpose regardless of the opposition or non-co-operation of men. If Israel will not respond, says John the Baptist, God is able from the very stones of the earth to raise up children to Abraham. God will redeem a people for his own possession; if the

The Implications of Repentance 85

chosen people refuse the opportunity, it will be offered to others.

Jesus confirmed these words of John on numerous occasions. When a Roman centurion exhibited a faith surpassing anything he had found in Israel, Jesus said, "I say unto you, that many shall come from the east and the west, and shall sit down with Abraham, and Isaac, and Jacob, in the kingdom of heaven: but the sons of the kingdom shall be cast forth into the outer darkness: there shall be the weeping and the gnashing of teeth" (Matt. 8:11, 12). When the chosen guests for the wedding feast spurn the invitation to attend, the invitations are not withdrawn; they are issued to others. The crossroads and the hedges are combed; the poor, the maimed, the lame, and the blind are brought in (Matt. 22:1-14; Luke 14:16-24). Religious privilege then as now sometimes resulted in pride of privilege with refusal to respond to the corresponding obligation. The cities which saw most of the mighty works of Jesus remained unrepentant. Tyre, Sidon, and Sodom, according to Jesus, would have been far more responsive had they had such opportunities. The Church must divest itself of all pride of privilege as it faces the demands of the new day. Wherever any branch of the Church fails to do so, God, we believe, will set it aside and raise up other agencies to work out his purposes. Our minds must not turn backward to glory in an honorable history; we must prepare for the stresses and pangs of the birth of a new world. If we refuse, God will use others.

"My Father worketh even until now," said Jesus, "and I work" (John 5:17). Jesus had just healed a man of his infirmity, so this remark should be set in that context. God is ceaselessly active healing the infirmities of mankind. Infirmities are as universal as the race; the most acute, sometimes unnoticed, are those of the soul, of the mind. Our world situation thunders at us that we must adjust our thinking to a Christian pattern or go out into the night. God has no especial pets among nations or individuals. He uses and blesses those who respond to his purposes; he sets aside those who will not and selects others to carry out his will. Some are placed in more strategic positions than others, with a correspondingly higher obligation.

The Apostle Paul frequently reminds us that God's purpose keeps moving forward even though men resist it. When Israel rejected the Gospel, the door of faith was opened to the Gentiles. The Gentiles' faith will "provoke them to jealousy" and ultimately God will redeem both Jew and Gentile. The day is past when we, as Christians, can talk of superior races and inferior races. Some peoples have had larger opportunities to develop their potentialities than others, but in Christ "there cannot be Greek and Jew, circumcision and uncircumcision, barbarian, Scythian, bondman, freeman; but Christ is all, and in all " (Col. 3:11). The Kagawas, the Sadhu Sundar Singhs, the Aggreys of Africa have demonstrated to us the quality of manhood that other races can produce in Christ Jesus. The Church has been painfully slow in recognizing these truths; it should have repented long ago on this point as well as others. The " middle wall of partition " of special privilege for certain races was broken down in the Christ on the cross. Our world must face this fact and work out a solution. The winning of the war will precipitate this problem into our laps. It is then that we shall face the greatest test that man has ever faced. Revenge on the conquered or wire-pulling for special privileges among the victors will set the stage for a new conflict more disastrous, if possible, than this one. The mind of the flesh will prompt us, as one of the stronger nations, to play for large advantages for ourselves; the mind of Christ will lead us to recognize that the small nations and the backward races have every right to develop their own potentialities to their fullest extent. We must be ready to help them do this.

The Church faces the greatest opportunity of its history to prepare public opinion for the new day. We must not only say to our people that God's purpose moves forward through history in spite of all opposition, but we must also say that that purpose is universal. God's black children, his brown children, and his yellow children are just as precious in his sight as his white children. Sentimentally we have recognized this. We have all been willing to concede this to be true after we all get to heaven, where maybe some bleaching will have been done. But should this life be excluded? It was for this life that Paul said that racial distinction was wiped out in Christ. There has long been need for repentance at this point.

It is quite doubtful if God is satisfied to have millions of his children underfed while others are overfed. Dives probably philosophized that it was a part of the constitution of nature that he should be rich and Lazarus poor, but Jesus did not consider this an adequate answer. It will never be possible to make all mankind equally prosperous as long as there are differing degrees of energy, ambition, industry, and thrift. A family, containing at one time four able-bodied men, lived on a two-hundred-acre farm near my home. There were about sixty acres of very fertile bottom land on this farm, but these people could never keep the taxes paid. Every few years they went through some scheme of refinancing to save a farm which they had inherited. About a half mile away lies a ridge farm. The owner bought on faith this forty acres of thin land and has paid for it. He has lived comfortably and kept his house and outbuildings neat and in good

The Implications of Repentance

repair. The buildings on the other farm have been, for years, in a tumble-down condition. This is an unanswerable argument against compulsory communism; the drones would all like the other man to labor to feed them. What we need to plead for is the right and opportunity for every man to work for a decent livelihood. We have a long way to go in America, where the white employees in a large munitions plant can strike when twenty Negroes are hired to work in the same plant. There is a good deal of repenting needed in America.

The Apocalyptist envisions complete redemption as including a great multitude, which no man can number, drawn from every people, tongue, and nation. That truth has implications for this world too. The radio dins it into our ears daily that isolationism is a state of mind. Sydney, Auckland, and Cape Town are closer to America, by the lanes of communication, than was Corinth to Athens. We cannot escape reckoning with a world become a neighborhood.

While we speak of the universality of God's purpose, we must not forget its individuality. Paul knew a Saviour who loved him, and gave himself up for him. Jesus talked of a God by whom the very hairs of our head are numbered. The purposes of this God are always beneficent: " And we know that to them that love God all things work together for good, even to them that are called according to his purpose" (Rom. 8:28).

It is God who takes the initiative in establishing this redemptive relationship: "But of him [God] are ye in Christ Jesus, who was made unto us wisdom from God, and righteousness and sanctification, and redemption" (I Cor. 1:30). Wisdom from God, the mind of Christ, is the goal of the Church. This comes through our fellowship with Christ. When the goal is reached repentance is complete. Until then we are on a pilgrimage toward the mind of Christ. There is a wisdom that is earthly, sensual, devilish. This wisdom must not be allowed to prevail in the shaping of our new world.

Another feature of Jesus' teaching about God must be mentioned: God often triumphs through apparent defeat. This was the hardest lesson that the disciples had to learn. When Jesus "began to teach them, that the Son of man must suffer many things, and be rejected by the elders, and the chief priests, and the scribes, and be killed, and after three days rise again" (Mark 8:31), it was too much for Peter who, no doubt, voiced the sentiments of the group. His rebuke of Jesus was met by the reply, "Get thee behind me, Satan; for thou mindest not the things of God, but the things of men" (Mark 8:33). This quotation illustrates perfectly the New Testament idea of repent-

The Implications of Repentance

ance. God and man have radically different viewpoints; before man ever understands the Kingdom he must get something of God's outlook. Peter's vision was clear as long as things were going well. The Transfiguration, with its attendant glory, convinced him of Jesus' Messiahship, but the idea of the Messiah's suffering and being rejected upset him terribly. From this it is easy to understand why the "word of the cross" was a stumbling stone to the Jew. Paul knew only too well the heartache and offense that it had caused him.

The Church in America has lived comfortably and lazily so long that we have almost forgotten that the Cross is central in our faith. Too often Christianity has been a religion of convenience and convention. The God of the Christian faith has never announced any such program of redemption. Possibly the Church in America needs a catacomb experience. Would we understand it, if it came? I believe millions would rise to meet it triumphantly, but why wait to exhibit our faith? There are other ways than martyrdom to sacrifice for the Kingdom.

Man

One's idea of man is inevitably determined by one's idea of God. Paul reminds us (Rom. 3:29, 30) that if one is a logical monotheist, he must believe that God is the God of both Jew and Gentile; otherwise we have tribal gods and polytheism. In the same sermon in which Paul described the Christian Era as a time when God demands that all men everywhere repent, he also said that "he made of one every nation of men to dwell on all the face of the earth, having determined their appointed seasons, and the bounds of their habitation; that they should seek God, if haply they might feel after him and find him, though he is not far from each one of us: for in him we live, and move, and have our being" (Acts 17:26–28a). It was revolutionary doctrine for the first century to teach that all men are of one blood. It was amazing for a Jew to teach this doctrine. Paul, having gone through the mental revolution called repentance, could now view the human race as God did. Has the Church of the twentieth century really risen to this viewpoint? It has not been long since we talked glibly of the "white man's burden," while we helped ourselves to the brown man's oil, tin, and rubber. Christian capital would never have yielded 50 per cent on an investment, while paying out wages of eight cents a day, if we had really believed that all men are of one blood. Funds given to charity out of such earnings did not cancel the need for repentance. Such profits would never have been made if the investor had looked at men as God does.

The Implications of Repentance 93

It came as a shock to the Early Church to learn that God is no respecter of persons. Peter expressed his amazement after Cornelius, the Roman, had told of his experience in prayer: "Of a truth I perceive that God is no respecter of persons: but in every nation he that feareth him, and worketh righteousness, is acceptable to him" (Acts 10:34, 35). Peter had been prepared for this new discovery by a vision: he was not to call common or unclean anything that God had cleansed, even though it be a Gentile's heart. Fortified by these words, Peter went to Cornelius, but upon entering the house he apologized for his actions, although they were in obedience to God's direct commands: "Ye yourselves know how it is an unlawful thing for a man that is a Jew to join himself or come unto one of another nation; and yet unto me hath God showed that I should not call any man common or unclean: wherefore also I came without gainsaying, when I was sent for" (Acts 10:28, 29). How often since Peter's experience have religious prejudices or traditions, or social conventions made us hesitate to follow the clear leading of God! Where this is yet true, we must return to the New Testament to get our directions.

Peter seemed to think that God was pursuing a rather doubtful course of action, yet felt that he should "go along." But Peter learned his lesson more readily than many of his Christian brethren, for upon his return to Jerusalem they contended with him: "Thou wentest in to men uncircumcised, and didst eat with them" (Acts 11:3). Peter's defense was that "the Spirit bade me go with them, making no distinction. . . . And as I began to speak, the Holy Spirit fell on them, even as on us at the beginning. And I remembered the word of the Lord, how he said, John indeed baptized with water; but ye shall be baptized with the Holy Spirit. If then God gave unto them the like gift as he did also unto us, when we believed on the Lord Jesus Christ, who was I, that I could withstand God?" (Acts 11:12, 15-17, and marg.). It was man's prejudice against God's purpose that day. It has frequently been so since. Only repentance can prevent our prejudices from opposing God's purposes for our world.

We are told that when Peter's critics "heard these things, they held their peace, and glorified God, saying, Then to the Gentiles also hath God granted repentance unto life" (Acts 11:18). They dubiously conceded the point, for these Judaistic Christians seem to have had reservations in their minds, as though they had said, "Well, that's all right for this once. God seems to have got you into this mess, but don't let anything like this happen again." At any rate, when the Gentile mission in Antioch was prospering too much, Jerusalem became greatly disturbed and even Peter, who had defended his actions in the case of Cornelius, on the ground that they were God-directed, now turned his back on the vision (Gal. 2:11–14). Such is the force of prejudice; such is the power of resistance to a new idea. Repentance, in the New Testament sense, is the only remedy for such human frailties.

Jesus had set the stage for events like the conversion of Cornelius. His first recorded preaching at Nazareth precipitated the issue. His old neighbors "wondered at the words of grace which proceeded out of his mouth" (Luke 4:16–30), but when he touched on an unpopular subject they sneered, "Is not this Joseph's son?" When Jesus saw that his message was rejected, he reminded them that lack of faith was not new among the chosen people. In the days of Elijah, when famine stalked the land for three and one half years, it was only the widow of Zarephath, a Gentile, who had faith enough to receive the bounty of God. Again, in the days of Elisha, when there were many lepers in Israel, only Naaman the Syrian, one of the conquering enemy, had faith enough to be healed. Such talk did not lie well on the stomachs of Nazareth, so "they were all filled with wrath in the synagogue, as they heard these things; and they rose up, and cast him forth out of the city, and led him unto the brow of the hill whereon their city was built, that they might throw him down headlong."

This was the community in which Jesus had increased "in favor with God and men." A gracious, beneficent personality may be quite acceptable in a sinful community as long as he does not interfere with its way of thinking and living. As a carpenter Jesus was liked: he did good, honest work; his charges were moderate; and no doubt he had a friendly word for all. But as a prophet he aroused fanatical indignation, for he condemned sin without fear or favor. He rebuked the stubborn unbelief of his own people, and applauded faith in every heart where it occurred. To his neighbors there could be no virtue in anyone of another race, unless he were a proselyte. These words about Naaman the Syrian, and the widow of Zarephath were fighting words.

Other incidents, such as that of the Syrophoenician woman, reflected badly on Jesus' own people. Jesus commended her faith: " O woman, great is thy faith: be it done unto thee even as thou wilt " (Matt. 15:28). In like manner, he said to the centurion of Capernaum, "Verily I say unto you, I have not found so great faith, no, not in Israel " (Matt. 8:10). The spiritually underprivileged often were eager for the crumbs that fell from the table, but God's own people scorned the invitation to the wedding feast of his Son.

Jesus found constant and uncompromising resistance to the idea that his own people might be rejected of God. When a man or a nation has had opportunity to solidify a prejudice, it is very difficult to break it down. Cadoux [48] thinks that this fact explains Jesus' use of parables; they are either for attack or defense. He says, " A parable often hides the truth until it is too late for the hearer to guard himself against it: it tells men in a story what they will not listen to in plain language, and therefore the incidence must not be clear until the end of the story is reached."

The parable of the Good Samaritan, for instance, attacks the self-satisfied racial superiority of the scribes and Pharisees. It was too late for the lawyer to defend himself, or his own religious group, when he saw how the parable commended the Samaritan and condemned his own religious leaders. Jesus slipped by his defenses before he could throw up his guard. The thought that Jesus considered a despised foreigner a better man than the professionally pious of the lawyer's own race was left to fester in his mind. The scribes needed to do a good deal of repenting on this point. The modern Church must seek the mind of Christ on these matters, for the mind of the scribes and Pharisees still appears in some circles.

This refusal of Israel to see that the Gentile might have a place in God's plan of redemption accounts for most of the persecution of Paul. Even near the end of his career, with all the Jews' accumulated ill will for him, "they were the more quiet" (Acts 22:2), as he spoke in the well-loved language of their fathers, but when he used the hated word "Gentiles," they angrily shouted, "Away with such a fellow from the earth: for it is not fit that he should live" (Acts 22:22), throwing off their garments and casting dust in the air.

This question of race was one upon which there was real need for repentance, for reversal of mind. Paul, as we have noted, laid down the principle that in Christ "there cannot be Greek and Jew, . . . barbarian, Scythian" (Col. 3:11). Peter had discovered that God is no respecter of races. With the Jews, as with us, new ideas came with much travail of soul. Well before the end of the first century they had, as a race, turned in disappointment from their Messiah because they could not accept such ideas. What this cost Paul, who at one time shared all their bitter contempt for the Gentile, is seen in his heartbroken wail: "I say the truth in Christ, I lie not, my conscience bearing witness with me in the Holy Spirit, that I have great sorrow and unceasing pain in my heart. For I could wish that I myself were anathema from Christ for my brethren's sake, my kinsmen according to the flesh" (Rom. 9:1–3). Repentance leaves no room for the racial theories of the first century — nor for those of Hitlerian Germany.

The ecumenical movement is undoubtedly in the direction of the mind of Christ, but it must pass beyond the stage of discussion. This calls for a long task of education.

Probably the most fruitful passage in which to study the implications of repentance is the Sermon on the Mount (Matt., chs. 5 to 7). It is not necessary, for the purpose of our discussion, to assume that the Sermon on the Mount is first chronologically in Jesus' teaching, or to assume that it is a single unified discourse. This much is certain: the author of our Gospel of Matthew felt that it was of strategic importance in Jesus' teaching, for it is the first teaching recorded after his words, "Repent ye; for the kingdom of heaven is at hand" (Matt. 4:17).

The opening note of the sermon is the key to happiness. Jesus invariably went straight to the heart of the issue before him. On this occasion he was confronted by a cross section of humanity: the multitude contained those sick of body, heart, and mind. Their hopes and fears, their questionings and aspirations, were typical of all humanity, so Jesus began to talk of happiness. No subject could have caught and held their attention more effectively.

But Jesus had some strange ideas of happiness; the

world had its own ideas on this subject. Jesus was out of line with these established conceptions:

"Blessed [happy] are the poor in spirit," said Jesus; "happy is the triumphant conqueror," thought the world.

"Blessed are they that mourn," said Jesus; "happy are they who enjoy life," thought the world.

"Blessed are the meek," said Jesus; "contemptible are the meek," thought the world.

"Blessed are they that hunger and thirst after righteousness," said Jesus; "eat, drink, and be merry," said the world.

"Blessed are the pure in heart," said Jesus; "happy are they who are satisfied with themselves," said the world.

Many Christians have genuine difficulty in feeling at home in the Beatitudes. We instinctively love their beautiful cadences, but when we think of their actual meaning for life they have a strange sound to our ears. We have to grow to their viewpoint; this is repentance. No man is born with the philosophy that the poor in spirit are blessed. Our natural impulse is not to rejoice in our utter dependence on God. We should much prefer to feel independent of him. Self-sufficiency apart from God is the dearest hope of the man who does not really know God. Surrendering our autonomy to God is the most difficult test that we

The Implications of Repentance

Christians ever undergo. Only the person who has made the absolute surrender and discovered the freedom and release that come from such surrender can understand what Jesus meant when he said, "Blessed are the poor in spirit: for theirs is the kingdom of heaven." They are in the Kingdom now: Jesus says, " theirs *is* the kingdom," not " theirs *shall be* the kingdom." After repentance we are capable of entering the Kingdom, participating in the reign of God's will. Then and then only can we understand the Kingdom ideas.

Only a mental revolution can enable one to appreciate Jesus' concept of happiness. Peter and John passed through such a revolution, for when they were beaten for preaching in the name of Jesus and allowed to go "they therefore departed from the presence of the council, rejoicing that they were counted worthy to suffer dishonor for the Name" (Acts 5:41). This is a far cry from the attitude that made them argue as to who should be greatest in the Kingdom, or to seek to call down fire from heaven upon men who did not receive the Saviour. Here we confront in the disciples two of the most common weaknesses of the Church: the desire for personal preferment, and the spirit of revenge upon those who do not agree with us. What a sorry tale could be told of ecclesiastical scrambling for honors, and of the jealousy and heartache on the part of men who do not receive the recognition they crave! How often the cause of Christ has been discredited by our attitude toward those who do not see things as we see them! In these two areas lies a most urgent need for repentance.

Paul, having got something of the mind of Christ, picked up somewhere a saying of the Saviour's that the four Evangelists had all overlooked: "It is more blessed to give than to receive." This became his philosophy: "In all things I gave you an example, that so laboring ye ought to help the weak, and to remember the words of the Lord Jesus, that he himself said, It is more blessed to give than to receive" (Acts 20:35). Why did this saying escape the attention of the Evangelists? Probably it did not seem to be very significant. Since the human mind is something like a sieve, the apparently unimportant falls through and is lost. The revolution in Paul's life produced a revolution in his thinking, causing him to see the importance of this saying and to preserve it.

Many professing Christians apparently do not believe that it is more blessed to give than to receive, so most of life's endeavor is a matter of getting and spending or hoarding. Man's acquisitive instinct is very strong. The more substantial element in society has normally striven for full storehouses and barns. When they bulge with bounty we are all inclined to

The Implications of Repentance

say, "Soul, . . . take thine ease." Jesus corrects this philosophy by reminding us that "a man's life consisteth not in the abundance of the things which he possesseth" (Luke 12:15). The postwar world may force us to a realization of this truth. Our worldly prosperity will undoubtedly be drastically affected. If we live and move and have our being in things, we shall feel greatly cramped in our "brave new world." If we discover the secret of the abundant life — the life that is eternal both here and there — we may really discover our souls in the days that lie ahead.

We have taken the Saviour's appraisal of giving and getting in mild, homeopathic doses:

> "Give a little, live a little, try a little mirth;
> Sing a little, bring a little happiness to earth.
> Pray a little, play a little, be a little glad;
> Rest a little, jest a little, if the heart is sad;
> Spend a little, send a little to another's door;
> Give a little, live a little, love a little more." [49]

This poem was written for a comfortable world. It has a kindly, pleasant sentiment, but "give a little" is a far cry from "God so loved the world, that he gave his only begotten son" (John 3:16). In the same manner, "love a little" is a far cry from "greater love hath no man than this, that a man lay down his life for his friends" (John 15:13). Probably the greatest defect in the Christian Church is that we have sought refuge from the high demands of the Christian faith in gentle sentiments. Our day calls for heroism, for daring, for sacrifice.

Jesus treated this matter seriously: "For whosoever would save his life shall lose it: and whosoever shall lose his life for my sake shall find it" (Matt. 16:25). We seem to expect to find the fullness of the Christian life by giving a few nickels to the Church and refraining from the grosser sins, but this does not make life very exciting.

What God Expects of Man

Most of the Sermon on the Mount deals with what God expects of man. The religious practices of that day fell into three classes — almsgiving, prayer, and fasting. Men had wrong ideas about all these. There is a message for our day also in Jesus' words.

Almsgiving (Matt. 6:2–4) and philanthropy had become a publicity stunt, a sounding of the trumpet to call attention to the generosity of the giver. Such men, said Jesus, have received their reward in full when men have seen their ostentatious giving. Alms should be given to aid the recipient, not to advertise the donor. Real religion calls upon men to help the

The Implications of Repentance

needy — "to visit the fatherless and widows in their affliction" (James 1:27) — but it must be so done as to meet their need, not to feed the giver's pride.

The prayer practices of the day were criticized by Jesus with especial severity. The hypocrites who love to "strike a pose" and pray in the synagogues and on the corners of the streets, that they may be seen of men; the Gentiles who think that they shall be heard for their much speaking, their repetitious religious chatter; the rapacious scribe who forecloses a mortgage on a widow's house, and, as a cloak for his rapacity, makes long prayers (Matt. 6:5-8; Mark 12:38-40), have all missed the purpose of prayer. Prayer is not to advertise the worshiper; it is not a method of wheedling a reluctant God; it is not a means of concealing one's rascality. Prayer (Matt. 6:9-13) is primarily praise and thanksgiving to God, and adoration of his holy name. It is, next, petition for the coming of his Kingdom, for our daily needs, for the pardon of our sins, and for deliverance from temptation. Christian prayer has simplicity and sincerity, directness and dignity. It was the conviction that Jesus had found a secret of prayer that other praying men did not know which led his disciples to say, "Lord, teach us to pray" (Luke 11:1).

The supreme caricature of Pharisaic prayer is found in the story of the Pharisee and the Publican (Luke

18:9–14). The Pharisee was not really praying; he was calling God's attention to his virtues. The description, "Prayed thus with himself," was a very clever way of telling the Pharisee that the center of interest in his prayer, in fact in all his religion, was himself, not God. The publican really prayed and got his answer. This parable enabled Jesus to say to the Pharisees that to which they would never have listened if he had made a direct attack on their ideas of prayer. His shaft went home before they saw his purpose.

If men have wrong ideas of prayer, they must reverse their minds to bring them into line with God's purposes. To participate in the Kingdom, man must put God in the center of his prayer.

Pharisaic notions of fasting also needed correction. They had made this form of self-discipline an occasion for mourning and disfigurement of face, that they might be seen of men to fast (Matt. 6:16–18). As in the case of almsgiving and prayer, the purpose was publicity. Jesus taught that fasting was to be directed toward God and that it was to be joyful. It seemed to be characteristic of him and his disciples not to fast at all (Mark 2:18–22).

The wrong note which pervaded the entire religious observance of the time was that publicity was the object of the worshiper. To enter the Kingdom, such worshipers must repent; they must reverse the pattern of their worship. Worship is for fellowship with God, not for the advertisement of one's piety.

Jesus set before his hearers a new concept of the Law and its demands. So radical was the new approach, as we have noted before, that he said, " Think not that I came to destroy the law or the prophets " (Matt. 5:17). Probably the best direction finder for Jesus' thought on this point lies in his words: " I desire mercy, and not sacrifice " (Matt. 9:13). Hosea (Hos. 6:6) had given these words eight centuries before as the gist of God's demands upon men. Jesus endorses them as embodying the heart of his own message.

Jesus' teaching was always in line with the best in the prophets, but he usually carried their noble insights even farther than they did. Hosea rebuked a corrupt, religious formalism which would substitute routine offerings of sacrificial animals for justice and decency in the lives of the worshipers. Jesus, in quoting Hosea, rebuked the narrow self-righteousness of the religious leaders which would prevent the spiritually disenfranchised from receiving the benefits of religion.

In Jesus' mouth the words, " I desire mercy, and not sacrifice," drew a line between the two great emphases in religion. This line might be called the Great Divide of all the faiths of mankind. On one side everything flows in the direction of legalism, ceremony, ritual. The all-important thing is how the forms of religion are carried out. Many lengthy controversies have been carried on in the Christian Church over forms and polity. Not only have these things divided the Church, but they have misdirected its energies. Many failures and tragedies have grown out of this fact. On the other side of the Great Divide all streams flow in the direction of human welfare, character, righteousness.

How often Jesus brushes aside man-made traditions in religion! "The sabbath was made for man, and not man for the sabbath" (Mark 2:27), he said. The Sabbath was not created so that man would have some Sabbatical rules to observe, but rather that man should have respite from toil and leisure for worship. Jesus frequently "broke the Sabbath" to heal and to help, because mankind is more important in God's eyes than an institution. In other ways Jesus treated with scant respect the traditions of men encrusted about true religion. The Church needs to return constantly to its New Testament to check the direction of its emphasis. When it does so, it will find numerous occasions to repent.

We still have those who shut the doors of heaven against all who have not been baptized in the right way. One of our church colleges, with a long and

The Implications of Repentance

honorable tradition, has just been dragged through a battle of years' duration over the manner in which its president, " a most excellent administrator and educator," had been baptized. The form was right, but it was executed by the wrong crowd. These things are tragic, because of the bitter feelings aroused between Christian men, but much more so because they obscure the real meaning of Christian baptism. Nothing would do the Church Universal more good than to lay aside some of the traditions of men which now divide and misdirect our efforts. We should seek the mind of Christ in the placing of our emphasis for the new day.

One of the most urgent needs for repentance lies in the sphere of American denominationalism. As a more or less typical example of our Southland, I wish to cite the case of a village of three hundred people which boasted (?) five Protestant churches. The Presbyterian minister received the largest salary of any of the five pastors — the munificent sum of nine hundred dollars a year. Of the five churches, no one had a live program: the situation forbade it. We all need to repent and " bring forth . . . fruits worthy of repentance "; then such situations cannot exist. What a rich life a minister might have as pastor of this entire village! What a heartbreaking experience to compete with four other men for a following in such a place! Is this not a great challenge to our denominational leaders?

We need a new concept of righteousness; this will give us a new concept of the Church. Many of us still go to the Old Testament for our idea of righteousness.

To the Hebrews of the first century the Law was eternal, perfect, and all-sufficient; righteousness was acquired by keeping it. The Law was too sacred to be defiled by teaching it to the uncircumcised. If the Law should prove too hard to keep, it was sufficient merely to hear it read. It was to such men that Paul said, "For not the hearers of the law are righteous before God, but the doers of the law shall be justified" (Rom. 2:13, and marg.). Even a Gentile who keeps the Law is better than a Jew who does not, said Paul.

Jesus, according to the Sermon on the Mount, offered a new concept of the Law, and, therefore, of righteousness: "Ye have heard that it was said to them of old time, Thou shalt not kill; and whosoever shall kill shall be in danger of the judgment: but I say unto you, that every one who is angry with his brother shall be in danger of the judgment; and whosoever shall say to his brother, Raca, shall be in danger of the council; and whosoever shall say, Thou fool, shall be in danger of the hell of fire" (Matt. 5:21, 22). This

The Implications of Repentance

was Jesus' graphic way of saying that the law against murder also forbids anger and contempt. Evil motives are just as sinful as evil deeds. For the Pharisee, this was a revolutionary thought.

The Authorized Version translates this passage: "Whosoever is angry with his brother without a cause." The words "without a cause" are not in the best MSS. of Matthew. They are an interpolation, growing out of a perfectly human impulse to tone down a hard saying. This is a good example of wresting the Kingdom ideas by force.

There are a good many examples of this in textual criticism; e.g., there is a refrain recurring in Matt. 6:4, 6, 18 (A.V.): "And thy Father which seeth in secret himself shall reward thee openly." The word "openly" does not occur in the best MSS., which read, "And thy Father who seeth in secret shall reward thee." It is an unregenerate instinct to desire that our praise be public, but this is just the sort of self-advertisement in religion that Jesus was condemning in this portion of the Sermon on the Mount. Repentance calls for the regeneration of the instinct for self-display. Another example of such wresting is found in I Cor. 13: 4, 5, where the Authorized Version reads, "Charity . . . is not easily provoked." The Revised Version (1901) follows the best MSS. in reading, "Love . . . is not provoked." "This is a hard saying; who can hear it?" For who has not been provoked with those whom he professes to love? It was inevitable that some scribe should endeavor to soften such a high demand. But it should stand to remind us that what we call "love" is often self-love, which is very easily provoked. Repentance gives us the right perspective here.

Returning to the Sermon on the Mount, Jesus went farther tŏ say that anger and contempt disqualify one for worship, until one has made good the offense to one's brother. In like manner (Matt. 5:27–32) adultery may be in the mind and in the heart, making one just as guilty as the overt act. Repentance prepares one to face the fact that evil motives bring guilt to men, even though they never flower into evil actions. The most drastic measures must be used to avoid offense, even to the loss of an eye or a hand.

The Old Testament (Lev. 19:12) forbade perjury. Jesus insisted that swearing should not be necessary at all: " Let your speech be, Yea, yea; Nay, nay " (Matt. 5:37). An honest man's "yes" or "no" should be enough. For the old *lex talionis*, " An eye for an eye, and a tooth for a tooth," Jesus substituted turning the other cheek (Matt. 5:38–42). The Old Testament had said, " Thou shalt love thy neighbor as thyself " (Lev. 19:18). The rabbinical emendation, " And hate thine enemy," Jesus corrected and

The Implications of Repentance 113

replaced with, "Love your enemies, and pray for them that persecute you." To this he added, "That ye may be sons of your Father who is in heaven" (Matt. 5:43-45). There must be a change of mind toward one's enemies if one would share in God's household. This is the old challenge, "Repent ye; for the kingdom of heaven is at hand," but in new form. There is no way to understand the Kingdom, much less enter it, without this mental transfiguration.

Scribal and Pharisaic mentality never approached this concept of righteousness. Hence, Jesus said, "Except your righteousness shall exceed the righteousness of the scribes and Pharisees, ye shall in no wise enter into the kingdom of heaven" (Matt. 5:20).

One example must suffice to illustrate the apostles' corrective emphasis on what constitutes true righteousness. Paul, a man who had advanced in his old religion beyond many of his own age, sat down in a kindly, grateful mood to write a "thank-you note" to his friends at Philippi. In process of writing, his mind turned to his former faith and its significance, as compared to his Christian faith. No man, he said, could outdistance him in religious heritage or religious achievement: "If any other man thinketh to have confidence in the flesh, I yet more: circumcised the eighth day, of the stock of Israel, of the tribe of

Benjamin, a Hebrew of Hebrews; as touching the law, a Pharisee; as touching zeal, persecuting the church; as touching the righteousness which is in the law, found blameless " (Phil. 3:4–6). But to Paul, from his new viewpoint, all this was a spiritual liability.

This was his definite and final decision: " Howbeit what things were gain to me, these have I counted loss for Christ. Yea verily, and I count all things to be loss for the excellency of the knowledge of Christ Jesus my Lord: for whom I suffered the loss of all things, and do count them but refuse, that I may gain Christ, and be found in him, not having a righteousness of mine own, even that which is of the law, but that which is through faith in Christ, the righteousness which is from God by faith " (Phil. 3:7–9). Paul had discovered a new righteousness that came direct from God through faith; from the new viewpoint the old righteousness was simply refuse. Paul was eager to forget all his personal achievements in religion: " That I may know him, and the power of his resurrection, and the fellowship of his sufferings, becoming conformed unto his death; if by any means I may attain unto the resurrection from the dead " (Phil. 3:10, 11). This new concept of righteousness was the result of a mental revolution in Paul; it was the result of repentance. Salvation is by grace through faith, not of works, in order that no man should glory.

The Implications of Repentance

The spirit which thanks God that one is better than other men is forever condemned and contemned.

Closely related to what God expects of men is the nature of his Kingdom and his manner of establishing it.

The Nature of the Kingdom

No theme was more central to Jewish thought than the Kingdom. From the teaching of the New Testament, it is clear that its writers felt that most men did not understand the Kingdom.

The people expected a kingdom on a Maccabean pattern, but on a grander and more permanent scale. As Jesus went about teaching in their synagogues, preaching the good news of the Kingdom, he associated it with " healing all manner of disease and all manner of sickness among the people " (Matt. 4:23). Soon after the temptation, "he came to Nazareth, where he had been brought up: and he entered, as his custom was, into the synagogue on the sabbath day, and stood up to read. And there was delivered unto him the book of the prophet Isaiah. And he opened the book, and found the place where it was written,

> The Spirit of the Lord is upon me,
> Because he anointed me to preach good tidings to the poor:

He hath sent me to proclaim release to the captives,
And recovering of sight to the blind,
To set at liberty them that are bruised,
To proclaim the acceptable year of the Lord.

And he closed the book, and gave it back to the attendant, and sat down: and the eyes of all in the synagogue were fastened on him. And he began to say unto them, To-day hath this scripture been fulfilled in your ears" (Luke 4:16–21). As he proceeded to preach, his fellow townsmen " wondered at the words of grace which proceeded out of his mouth" (Luke 4:22). This, according to Luke, was Jesus' conception of preaching the Kingdom of God: not the battle cry of the warrior was characteristic of this Kingdom, but the words of grace from the lips of a Redeemer; not conquest and captives, but release of captives and the setting free of those that were bruised constituted his program for the Kingdom.

But these words of grace found no welcome in the hearts of his fellow citizens. Because he taught that other peoples might share in the grace of God, his words kindled murderous passions (Luke 4:29) where gracious sentiments should have grown. The Kingdom was not for the conqueror, but for the poor in spirit (Matt. 5:3), for the persecuted who suffered for righteousness' sake (Matt. 5:10). As I have said

The Implications of Repentance

previously, misfortune was regarded as a judgment of God upon sin. Towers fell on men because they were sinners (Luke 13:4, 5), not because the towers were poorly constructed. Men were murdered at worship, because they had sinned (Luke 13:1–3), not because they lived under a jackal of a tyrant. Children were born blind because they had sinned prenatally; or, perchance, one or both parents had sinned (John 9:1–3).

Jesus was constantly correcting such ideas. Much of Old Testament theology assumed that prosperity was a mark of God's favor, that adversity was proof of his disfavor. The fact that The Book of Job and other Old Testament voices had repudiated this brand of theology was not enough. In fact, Jesus' repudiation was not sufficient to correct this error. There are Christians today who still think in the pre-Christian pattern.

The Kingdom is not for pious talkers, nor for the socially secure and respectable, the rich and influential, and it is not secured by heredity. "Not every one that saith unto me, Lord, Lord, shall enter into the kingdom of heaven; but he that doeth the will of my Father who is in heaven" (Matt. 7:21). When a "certain ruler" went away sorrowful because the demands of the Kingdom were too hard, Jesus said, "How hardly shall they that have riches enter into the kingdom of God! For it is easier for a camel to enter in through a needle's eye, than for a rich man to enter into the kingdom of God" (Luke 18:24, 25). The revolutionary nature of this statement is reflected in the amazed response of those who heard it: "Then who can be saved?" (Luke 18:26.) Matthew (Matt. 19:25) records that the disciples "were astonished exceedingly, saying, Who then can be saved?" If the rich, who have the leisure to be religious, are saved with such difficulty, what chance does the poor man have?

Again, descent from Abraham, contrary to popular theology, was not sufficient to admit one to the Kingdom. Even Gentiles shall displace unworthy Jews (Matt. 8:11, 12). Even publicans and harlots shall enter the Kingdom before "the chief priests and the elders of the people" (Matt. 21:23-32), who say, "I go, sir" and do not. Professional religionists may be less responsive to God than open sinners: "The publicans and the harlots believed him [John]: and ye, when ye saw it, did not even repent yourselves afterward, that ye might believe him" (Matt. 21:32). These words stung to the quick and were accepted as a challenge to battle.

Since the first invited guests, the religiously privileged, with one consent made excuse, God would supply guests for the Kingdom from the religiously

The Implications of Repentance

disenfranchised, " the poor and maimed and blind and lame " (Luke 14:15–24). It is the little children to whom the Kingdom belongs (Luke 18:16). Even a Nicodemus, a ruler of the Jews, must not only be born again to enter the Kingdom, but his spiritual sight must be cleared before he understands the Kingdom. As a teacher of Israel, he should have understood these things (John 3:10). " Whosoever shall not receive the kingdom of God as a little child, he shall in no wise enter therein " (Luke 18:17).

All this is the New Testament way of saying that there must be a transformation of mind, a transposition of values, a loss of a sense of one's own importance, before one can enter the Kingdom. That this is not easy is demonstrated by history and by religious experience. The first thing we assert and the last thing we surrender is our own sense of self-importance. The clash between the demands of the Kingdom and the ways of the human heart has supplied centuries of acute conflict.

I believe that it was in reference to this that Jesus said, " And from the days of John the Baptist until now the kingdom of heaven suffereth violence, and men of violence take it by force " (Matt. 11:12). I am confident that Thayer's interpretation of this passage is wrong: " The kingdom of heaven is taken by violence, carried by storm, i.e., a share in the heavenly

Kingdom is sought for with the most ardent zeal and the intensest exertion." [50] This sounds like a piece of Hegelian optimism, which is thoroughly refuted by the present temper of the world.

Never at any time, since the days of John the Baptist, have men of violence rushed ardently into the Kingdom. What the passage does mean is that the Kingdom of heaven is violently treated — it was in the days of John and Jesus and is yet — and men of violence wrest it to their own purposes. This is what the Greek, καὶ βιασταὶ ἁρπάζουσιν αὐτήν, normally means: "Violent men plunder it" to make the Kingdom serve their purposes. They may conceive of themselves as being in the Kingdom, of promoting its advancement; but they have come to the Kingdom with a set of ideas foreign to its ideals; therefore, the Kingdom must be forced to fit the pattern of the man and of the moment. Church history is strewn with examples of this, and so is Christian experience. It is a question of forcing the Kingdom or transforming the man. The ministry must face this issue.

The last point of emphasis regarding the nature of the Kingdom is the manner of its coming. Both Jesus and John said that it was imminent, at hand. But to those who "supposed that the kingdom of God was immediately to appear," Jesus told the parable of the Pounds: "A certain nobleman went into a far coun-

The Implications of Repentance

try, to receive for himself a kingdom, and to return" (Luke 19:11–26). Certainly one idea in this parable is that there will be delay in the full consummation of the Kingdom.

To the Pharisees who asked "when the kingdom of God cometh," he replied, "The kingdom of God cometh not with observation: neither shall they say, Lo, here! or, There! for lo, the kingdom of God is within you" (Luke 17:20, 21). The meaning of the preposition ἐντός, translated "within," is much disputed. The difficulty grows out of Jesus' saying that the Kingdom was in the Pharisees, his enemies. One school of interpreters takes it in the sense of "among." The Kingdom of God is "among" you. The lexical grounds for this interpretation are quite slender. Allen[51] suggests that the "you" is indefinite, as is common in Semitic speech, i.e., the Kingdom is an inner thing, not an external realm. Sledd[52] has suggested that ἐντός means "within" as it normally does, but that the reference is to the "group within the group"; i.e., out of the group represented by the Pharisees the nucleus of the Kingdom comes. One fact that seems clear is that the Kingdom will not burst full-blown overnight by some military exploit or some divine cataclysmic intervention. In line with this is the parable of the Ten Virgins.

The parables of the growth of the Kingdom clearly

bring out the thought of its silent, continuous, progressive coming. The parable of the Mustard Seed (Matt. 13:31, 32) stresses its small beginnings and its great growth; the parable of the Leaven (Matt. 13:33) pictures a silent, pervasive force working throughout the world until all is leavened.

Even after all Jesus' efforts to depict the coming of the Kingdom, his disciples still did not see the point. After the Resurrection, on the eve of the Ascension, they said, "Lord, dost thou at this time restore the kingdom to Israel?" (Acts 1:6.) It is Israel's kingdom, for Israel to run! It can be handed over to Israel, whether the nation is prepared for it or not! Israel's kingdom, not God's! Jesus replied to this honest but misguided question: "It is not for you to know times or seasons, which the Father hath set within his own authority. But ye shall receive power, when the Holy Spirit is come upon you: and ye shall be my witnesses both in Jerusalem, and in all Judæa and Samaria, and unto the uttermost part of the earth" (Acts 1:7, 8). According to Jesus, it was not the disciples' business to discover when the Kingdom of God was coming; it was their business to witness to him. The Kingdom will come without observation, as seed sown upon the earth springs up and grows, while the sower sleeps and rises night and day without understanding how the growth takes place (Mark

4:26–29). However, the fact that the growth is unseen and mysterious to the sower does not prevent the harvest: it is assured.

There were many things for the disciples to learn about the Kingdom. There are yet many for us to learn today. As God moves forward in establishing his Kingdom, he will use human instrumentalities. We must have his mind if we are to be usable in his hands.

For the mind of the flesh is death; but the mind of the Spirit is life and peace: because the mind of the flesh is enmity against God; for it is not subject to the law of God, neither indeed can it be: and they that are in the flesh cannot please God.—Rom. 8:6–8.

Have this mind in you, which was also in Christ Jesus: who, existing in the form of God, counted not the being on an equality with God a thing to be grasped, but emptied himself, taking the form of a servant, being made in the likeness of men; and being found in fashion as a man, he humbled himself, becoming obedient even unto death, yea, the death of the cross.
—Phil. 2:5–8.

4

THE TWO MINDS: THE MIND OF THE FLESH AND THE MIND OF CHRIST

The New Testament is the story of clashing viewpoints. This clash occurs along the entire front of human life and thought.

The Conflict Between the Two Minds

In the Synoptic Gospels the clash is largely between the teachings of Jesus and the popular ideas of life and religion. As we have seen, it includes matter as diversified as one's personal attitude on race; the secret of happiness; and the nature of God's Kingdom.

Jesus was constantly offering a corrective for the false notions in vogue in his day. When James and John asked for the places of honor in his Kingdom, he reminded them that they had the wrong idea of greatness: "Ye know that they who are accounted to rule over the Gentiles lord it over them; and their great ones exercise authority over [i.e., oppress] them. But it is not so among you: but whosoever would become great among you, shall be your minister; and whosoever would be first among you, shall be servant of all. For the Son of man also came not to be ministered unto, but to minister, and to give his life a ransom for many" (Mark 10:42–45). In other words, the pagan pattern for greatness is just the reverse of greatness in the Kingdom of God. In the eyes of the world, the domineering are great; to Jesus, those who serve are great. He offers his own life as the pattern for true greatness.

The nature of defilement, the validity of religious ritual, and the menace of split loyalty come in for discussion in Jesus' teaching. Conventional piety considered that neglect of ritual brought defilement; Jesus taught that evil thoughts and vicious words defile men (Mark 7:1–23).

Wordly prudence considered it wise to pay lip service to God, but to heap up for oneself treasures upon earth; Jesus said, "Ye cannot serve God and mammon" (Matt. 6:24). No man can serve two masters; some one thing must be sovereign in a man's life. Split loyalty is disloyalty to one or the other of the supposed masters.

In the Gospel of John, the clash centers around Jesus' person and his claims. The "Jews" challenge these claims every step of the way. Even Nathanael was frankly troubled over the humble origin of Jesus. He expressed his perplexity to Philip: "Can any good thing come out of Nazareth?" (John 1:46.) Surely the Messiah would not come from such a background! This doubt matured into convinced unbelief in the case of the majority of Jesus' own people: "And they said, Is not this Jesus, the son of Joseph, whose father and mother we know? how doth he now say, I am come down out of heaven?" (John 6:42.)

This play back and forth between faith and disbelief appears, again and again, in the Fourth Gospel: "And there was much murmuring among the multitudes concerning him: some said, He is a good man; others said, Not so, but he leadeth the multitude astray" (John 7:12). So bitter was the hatred that no one spoke openly of him "for fear of the Jews."

But the question as to who Jesus was would not down: "Some therefore of them of Jerusalem said, Is not this he whom they seek to kill? And lo, he speaketh openly, and they say nothing unto him. Can it be that the rulers indeed know that this is the Christ? Howbeit we know this man whence he is: but when the Christ cometh, no one knoweth whence he is" (John 7:25–27).

After Jesus healed the man born blind, the question came to the fore again: "Some therefore of the Pharisees said, This man is not from God, because he keepeth not the sabbath. But others said, How can a man that is a sinner do such signs? And there was a division among them" (John 9:16).

This question, as to who Jesus was, is never farther

away than just under the surface of the Gospel of John. Nicodemus voiced the judgment of the open-minded but cautious leaders: " Rabbi, we know that thou art a teacher come from God; for no one can do these signs that thou doest, except God be with him" (John 3:2). But the final verdict of the majority was rejection of him and his claims: " He came unto his own, and they that were his own received him not" (John 1:11).

The book of The Acts takes up the clash at this point. As we have already noticed in Chapter II, Peter emphatically insists on the contrast between God and the people in their treatment of Jesus, " The God of our fathers raised up Jesus, whom ye slew, hanging him on a tree. Him did God exalt with his right hand to be a Prince and a Saviour, to give repentance to Israel, and remission of sins" (Acts 5:30, 31). This quotation from Peter's preaching is typical of a number of others which could be cited to illustrate this clash of viewpoints.

In Stephen's sermon there is not only a clash of viewpoints, but also a clash of wills: " Ye stiffnecked and uncircumcised in heart and ears, ye do always resist the Holy Spirit: as your fathers did, so do ye. Which of the prophets did not your fathers persecute? and they killed them that showed before of the coming of the Righteous One; of whom ye have now become betrayers and murderers; ye who received the law as it was ordained by angels, and kept it not" (Acts 7:51-53).

These contradictory viewpoints appear repeatedly in the book of The Acts. Paul is the supreme example of one who, at one time or other, occupied an extreme position on each side of the question before the Jew. Before Damascus, he breathed "threatening and slaughter against the disciples of the Lord" (Acts 9:1); after Damascus, he said, "For to me to live is Christ" (Phil. 1:21). His actual experience as one who had held both viewpoints should make what he says on the subject especially enlightening.

Paul touched on almost every phase of life in his epistles, but the crux of all his thinking was the Cross. Here the clash occurred in its most violent form. Christ crucified was to the Jews a stumbling block, and to the Gentiles sheer silliness (I Cor. 1:23). Well did Paul know the transports of fury that the preaching of a crucified Messiah could arouse in a Jewish heart. He had felt its searing heat in his own heart. How often had he heard the cynical snicker of the Gentile when he had preached Christ crucified as the Lord and Saviour of all men!

But this world with its wisdom never came to know God until it believed the word of the Cross. Then he became "unto them that are called, both Jews and Greeks, Christ the power of God, and the wisdom of God" (I Cor. 1:24).

Paul spoke out of a personal experience that had been both bitter and radiant when he said, "The foolishness of God is wiser than men; and the weakness of God is stronger than men" (I Cor. 1:25). When he was going about to establish his own righteousness he, like his kinsmen in the flesh, did not submit himself to the righteousness of God. When he recognized that his own righteousness, self-righteousness, was simply refuse — an actual liability, spiritually — he gladly suffered the loss of all these things to gain Christ and be found in him, not having his own righteousness which comes from the law, but the righteousness which comes from God and rests on faith in Christ Jesus (Phil. 3:8, 9).

Here is the clue to the clashing viewpoints so apparent in the New Testament. When a man's religious thinking centers in himself, he is always out of harmony with God. When God is made the center of all one's thinking, one's aspirations, one's attitudes, then one's actions find a natural orbit around God's purpose. The chief difficulty with the Church seems to be that most Christian lives, like the ellipse, have two foci. As we try to make both God and self the directing center of life, we distort life. As the foci of an ellipse are moved closer together, the ellipse

The Two Minds 133

becomes more like a perfect circle; as they move farther apart, the ellipse is elongated and flattened out. So life becomes distorted when we try to include our own wills along with God's as the directing center of life.

If the Church would recognize what causes distorted Christian lives, it would be well on the way to find a cure. The secret lies in the surrender of the mind to the will of God. Canon Streeter wrote: "Clearly, any individual who has completely surrendered his will to God will have got rid of egocentric narcissism; one who has inwardly appropriated the teachings of Christ about anxiety for the morrow will have got rid of fear obsessions; one who has assimilated other aspects of the teaching of Christ will cease to be obsessed by sex or resentment; and so on. It will be objected that a large number of Christians have tried this, but the success of their endeavour — so far as can be judged by outward actions — has not been great. This barrenness of result, I would suggest, is mainly due to the fact that the subconscious depths of the personality have not been reached." [58]

The only remedy for obliquity in moral vision and for distortion of life lies in shifting the center of our thoughts and aspirations. The Christian faith alone enables one to do this. To quote again from Streeter: "Religion can overcome the egocentricity of man —

by inviting him to become the willing instrument of an Eternal Purpose, and then by giving him the insight and the power to be this. So long as a man's hopes, desires, and fears are primarily egocentric, it is impossible for him to take an objective view, not merely of the comparative rightness of different lines of conduct, but even of their practicability." [54]

The basic cause of this clash of viewpoints along the whole front of human life lies in what Paul calls "the mind of the flesh."

The Mind of the Flesh

Paul speaks of two characteristics of the mind of the flesh: unwillingness to be subject to the law of God, and inability to be (Rom. 8:6, 7). The word "mind," φρόνημα, which Paul uses here, suggests the "bent of one's mind," one's inclinations. These inclinations are marked by hostility to God and revolt against the law of God. It is this revolt of the natural man that makes the Pauline doctrine of reconciliation necessary. This will be discussed more fully in the next chapter.

The unwillingness of man to be subject to the law of God explains why Jesus demanded repentance as a preparation for the coming Kingdom. A kingdom, with its subjects in revolt, could have neither stability nor peace. Men must reverse their minds before they

The Two Minds

can participate in God's reign. Without this, they are subversive elements in the Kingdom — enemies, not citizens.

The inability of the mind of the flesh to be subject to the law of God suggests the necessity for the Johannine formula: "Except a man be born again" (John 3:3, A.V.). As stated previously, without the birth of a new nature, men — even religious leaders of the rank of Nicodemus — can neither comprehend nor participate in the reign of God. Does the fact of this inability suggest why the New Testament writers speak of God's *giving* repentance (Acts 11:18; II Tim. 2:25) unto men?

The phrase, "mind of the flesh," is peculiar to this passage (Rom. 8:6, 7). In fact, this word for mind, φρόνημα, occurs in only one other verse in the New Testament, Rom. 8:27. In this latter instance, it is "the mind of the Spirit." Here again we confront a clash of "minds." The mind dominated by the flesh leads to death, because of its hostility to God; the mind imparted by the Spirit leads to life and peace, for the mind of the Spirit is in harmony with God's mind, and makes intercession for man "according to the will of God" (Rom. 8:27).

The cognate verb, φρονέω, is almost exclusively a Pauline word. It always implies a deep-seated mental outlook. Of the twenty-seven occurrences in the

New Testament, twenty-four are in the Pauline epistles. One of the three instances not in the Pauline letters is addressed to Paul by the Jews of Rome when they said to him, "But we desire to hear of thee what thou thinkest: for as concerning this sect, it is known to us that everywhere it is spoken against" (Acts 28:22). Here is a clash of viewpoints on the nature of the Christian movement; the Jews of Rome want to know where Paul stands.

The remaining two instances not in the Pauline epistles occur in connection with Jesus' rebuke to Peter near Caesarea Philippi, when Jesus foretold his betrayal, crucifixion, and death. To Peter's shocked exclamation, "Mercy on thee, Lord: this shall never be unto thee," Jesus replied, "Get thee behind me, Satan: thou art a stumbling-block unto me: for thou mindest not the things of God, but the things of men" (Matt. 16:22, 23; Mark 8:32, 33). To Peter's mind, the death of Christ would be an unmitigated tragedy; to Christ, it was a fulfillment of God's purpose.

The Cross is the greatest difficulty that the natural man faces in the Christian faith. It is still the primary difficulty that the Jew faces in accepting Christ as Saviour. It is a difficulty that appears again and again in the New Testament. The mind of the flesh cannot understand a suffering Saviour.

Although the phrase, "the mind of the flesh," is

peculiar to Rom. 8:6, 7, the idea occurs in many places, expressed by a variety of phrases.

Paul spoke of a wisdom of the world that knew not God (I Cor. 1:21); of a wisdom of the rulers of this world who failed to know the "wisdom . . . which God foreordained before the worlds unto our glory: . . . for had they known it, they would not have crucified the Lord of glory" (I Cor. 2:7, 8); of a "fleshly wisdom" as a ground of glorying which he had rejected (II Cor. 1:12). He also spoke of man-made rules for ascetic practices "which . . . have . . . a show of wisdom in will-worship, and [mock] humility, and severity to the body; but are not of any value against the indulgence of the flesh" (Col. 2:23). These are all set in strong contrast with the wisdom imparted by God, with whom the wisdom of this world is foolishness (I Cor. 3:19), and who made Christ to be wisdom to us from God, and righteousness and sanctification to us and redemption (I Cor. 1:30). It is God's purpose to destroy the wisdom of the worldly-wise (I Cor. 1:19).

The offense of the Cross precipitates this discussion of the two wisdoms. As Nietzsche has said, "The idea of a God on the cross reversed all the values of antiquity."[55] To the Jew, a crucified Messiah was an odious thought, a stumbling block, a cause for bitterness of soul and bitterness of speech. To the Greek, the idea was a cause for derision, too ridiculous to take seriously. But a third group, those that were called, both Jews and Greeks, found in this message "Christ the power of God, and the wisdom of God" (I Cor. 1:24). The wisdom of the world is set in sharp contrast to the wisdom of God, and "the foolishness of God" was seen to be "wiser than men."

But a degree of maturity was required to see the relationship between the two wisdoms. The word of the Cross might be an occasion for blasphemy with the Jew and a cause for tittering with the Greek, but among them that were fullgrown, it was recognized as wisdom, "yet a wisdom not of this world, nor of the rulers of this world, who are coming to nought" (I Cor. 2:6). It was God's wisdom foreordained before the worlds. That which enabled men to know "the things that were freely given to us of God" (I Cor. 2:12) was the presence and teaching of the Spirit: "Now the natural man receiveth not the things of the Spirit of God: for they are foolishness unto him; and he cannot know them [the old inability of Rom. 8:6, 7 and John 3:3, 5], because they are spiritually judged" (I Cor. 2:14).

The natural man is defective at this point. Rebirth into a different order, a third race, where there is neither Greek nor Jew, is necessary for insight into these things. To those who were perishing, the Gospel was foolishness; to those who were being saved, it was "the power of God, and the wisdom of God."

The outcome of this defect was that the wise man of this world and the learned scribe were left by the wayside in unbelief. "Not many wise after the flesh, not many mighty, not many noble," were called. This is in line with the response of those who should have been guests at the Great Supper (Matt. 22:1–14).

The Epistle of James (James 3:15) speaks of a wisdom that cometh not down from above, "but is earthly, sensual, devilish." Its expression in society is bitter jealousy, faction, confusion, and every vile deed. This has been all too often illustrated in our world. "But the wisdom that is from above is first pure, then peaceable, gentle, easy to be entreated, full of mercy and good fruits, without variance, without hypocrisy" (James 3:17).

As we have seen, the core of the "mind of the flesh" is hostility to God and inability of itself to change. Its mood is expressed by opportunistic self-seeking, jealousy, quarrelsomeness, strife, confusion, and vicious living.[56] "The works of the flesh," says Paul, "are manifest, which are these: fornication, uncleanness, lasciviousness, idolatry, sorcery, enmities, strife, jealousies, wraths, factions, divisions, parties, envyings, drunkenness, revellings, and such like; of which I forewarn you, even as I did forewarn you, that they who practise such things shall not inherit the kingdom of God" (Gal. 5:19–21). The "mind of the flesh" and the phrase "in the flesh" are used synonymously by Paul, so we assume that the "works of the flesh" are the expression of the mind of the flesh (Rom. 8:6–8).

The inability of the mind of the flesh to submit to the will of God and therefore please him is met by the work of the Holy Spirit: "But the fruit of the Spirit is love, joy, peace, longsuffering, kindness, goodness, faithfulness, meekness, self-control" (Gal. 5:22, 23). The contrast between "works of the flesh" and "fruit of the Spirit" should be noted. Works suggest effort and striving; fruit suggests spontaneous growth, the expression of life. The plural "works," used by Paul, suggests diversity and disunity; the singular "fruit" suggests unity in achievement. These first impressions are borne out by the fact that the works of the flesh named by Paul are essentially divisive, while the fruit of the Spirit is unifying. The Christian graces, listed as the fruit of the Spirit, are essentially a unity of Christian virtue.

The inability of the mind of the flesh is further seen in the failure of the world's wise men and learned scribes to understand the "word of the cross," and to understand the things of the Spirit in general. Nicodemus, as we have noted, is only typical at this point: Except a man be born from above, by the Spirit, the

Kingdom of God is an enigma and an offense. He not only cannot understand it, but cannot participate in it, even in ignorance. In such a state, one may "have a zeal for God" (Rom. 10:2, 3), but be so bent on establishing his own righteousness that he becomes a rebel against God, as did Paul. Men of violence still attempt to wrest the Kingdom of heaven to make it fit in with their ideas. However, it is God's Kingdom and he has a way of carrying out his purposes whether we treat them violently or not. Kicking against the pricks does not seem to bring enlightenment; it rather brings resentment against those who have found the Way. Only a new light, a light above the brightness of the noonday sun, helps.

It is well to recall at this point that it was as God presented new light to the world in the Gospel that he also presented the challenge: "Repent ye," change your mind in the light of the new revelation. "The times of ignorance . . . God overlooked; but now he commandeth men that they should all everywhere repent" (Acts 17:30).

The Mind of Christ

The mind of Christ, according to Paul, represents a completely different attitude. Although he was on an equality with God, he did not grasp the privilege and exploit it for self, nor did he set up in opposition to the Father. On the contrary, he "emptied himself," by "taking the form of a servant," "and being found in fashion as a man, he humbled himself" further "even unto death," the most ignominious death that could be inflicted upon man (Phil. 2:5–11). When all his human nature recoiled from such a death, and he prayed that the cup pass from him, he conditioned the prayer upon its harmony with God's will: "My Father, if it be possible, let this cup pass away from me: nevertheless, not as I will but as thou wilt" (Matt. 26:39).

This opportunity for self-assertion on the part of Jesus is played upon in the New Testament. The Tempter used it in his approach to Jesus after the baptism: "If thou art the Son of God, command that these stones become bread" (Matt. 4:3). The force of the conditional clause in the Greek is practically causal: "Since you are the Son of God, command that these stones become bread." The appeal is, "Use your prerogatives to your own advantage." Satan's assumption is that of course all power is used for selfish ends.

This assumption lies very near the heart of The Book of Job: "Doth Job fear God for nought? Hast not thou made a hedge about him, and about his house, and about all that he hath, on every side? thou hast blessed the work of his hands, and his substance is increased in the land. But put forth thy hand now, and touch all that he hath, and he will renounce thee to thy face" (Job 1:9–11). Privilege, like power, is always used selfishly, so Satan assumed. Even in religion, a man's primary objective is to feather his own nest. When religion ceases to yield dividends, men will cease to be religious. "Doth Job fear God for nought?" According to Satan, Job was the original of the "rice Christian." This is the mind of the flesh exemplified; the ego is the center of all striving, all aspiring, all loyalty. The mind of Christ is the exact reverse.

The Transition Is Repentance

The change represented by the transition from this Satanic philosophy to that of Christ, who emptied himself, is the New Testament idea of repentance. The mind of Christ is patterned after the method of God's dealing with men: "God so loved the world, that he gave his only begotten Son" (John 3:16). Self-giving is the heart of one philosophy; self-protection is the heart of the other.

Jesus made his plea for repentance in varied language, but none was more arresting and forceful than when he said: "If any man would come after me, let him deny himself, and take up his cross, and follow me. For whosoever would save his life shall lose it: and whosoever shall lose his life for my sake shall find it" (Matt. 16:24, 25).

To deny self is not synonymous with self-denial. The latter can be too trivial to be serious. To deny self is to dethrone self. It is synonymous with taking up one's cross. Men did not normally take up crosses as burdens — Simon of Cyrene was an exception to this rule. The cross was the visible death sentence of the man who bore it. Dethroning self and taking up one's cross are two ways of saying the same thing: Self is no longer sovereign; Christ is sovereign. This is the basic fact of repentance.

The reason Jesus gave for this counsel was that "whosoever would save his life shall lose it." Self-assertion is the surest method of self-defeat. Self-dethronement is the way to self-realization of the highest sort: "Whosoever shall lose his life for my sake shall find it." One may "have" his life and never know the depth and meaning of life until it is surrendered to Christ.

> "Make me a captive, Lord,
> And then I shall be free;
> Force me to render up my sword,
> And I shall conqueror be.

"My will is not my own
  Till thou hast made it thine;
  If it would reach a monarch's throne
  It must its crown resign;

"It only stands unbent
  Amid the clashing strife,
  When on thy bosom it has leant,
  And found in thee its life." [57]

To put the idea in other words:

"That soul may last but never lives,
  Who much receives but nothing gives." [58]

The Apostle Paul spoke of the death of Christ from this viewpoint: "And he died for all, that they that live should no longer live unto themselves, but unto him who for their sakes died and rose again" (II Cor. 5:15). The preposition "unto" is used twice in this sentence to translate the dative case. The more correct preposition would be "for." Let us read the quotation, substituting "for" for "unto": "He died for all, that they that live should no longer live for themselves, but for him who for their sakes died and rose again." What a light this sheds on the doctrine of the atonement!

The atoning death of Christ was designed, in so far as it affected men, to put a stop to our living for self and to enable us to begin to live for him who died for us. But one will say: " Why should I live for another? My life is my own. I will live it as I see fit. Why should I live for Christ? " We see the reason in Jesus' words: " Whosoever would save his life shall lose it: and whosoever shall lose his life for my sake shall find it " (Matt. 16:25; cf. Mark 8:35; Luke 9:24).

These are the words of the One who said: " For the Son of man came to seek and to save that which was lost " (Luke 19:10). Does this imply that the mass of mankind is lost in self-seeking? " Not thy will, but mine, be done," is the protest of the unregenerate man. Much so-called Christian praying unconsciously seeks to conform God's will to the desires of the one praying. That is why most of us think of prayer in terms of asking God for the things we want. Repentance is the transition to the spirit which prays, " Not my will, but thine, be done." As long as we seek to have our way in the smallest detail of life, we need to " repent."

We have already seen that the same Saviour who came to seek and to save the lost came also to call sinners, which includes all mankind, according to the New Testament, to " repentance " (Luke 5:32). He came that men might have life and have it more abundantly (John 10:10). These are three ways of saying the same thing. Men are lost in self-seeking; they are found, when they come to themselves, in " repentance "; and this self-discovery, by losing self in Christ, is the abundant life.

I believe that the New Testament teaches the substitutionary atonement, but there are reaches of thought in the atonement that none of the doctrines formulated by men have yet explored. Too often the substitutionary atonement has been accepted in the spirit of " Jesus paid it all, so there is nothing for me to do." As I understand the atonement, in the light of II Cor. 5:15, Jesus paid it all, so I owe my all to him. Henceforth and forever, I live for him and not for myself. This transformation of mental outlook is the essence of repentance. To repeat, Jesus called for repentance because the Kingdom of heaven was at hand. No other attitude of mind admits one to the Kingdom; with no other attitude can one participate in or comprehend the Kingdom.

This change of mind is often accompanied by travail of soul. A complete reversal of one's standard of values is a soul-searching experience. The reorientation of one's life, with respect to both God and man, will not be accomplished by man's will unaided. The New Testament teaches that God takes the initiative in this reorientation. This will be discussed later.

The Reorientation of the Mind of Man

It must be said again that the transition from the mind of the flesh to the mind of Christ constitutes the New Testament concept of repentance. Self-assertion gives way to self-surrender to Christ. Hostility to God's purposes and rebellion against his providences are replaced by joyful obedience. Opportunism gives way to selfless service. The inability of the mind of the flesh to do God's will is offset by the empowering work of the Spirit. Man moves into a new world, with a new perspective. Coming out of darkness into light changes all the conditions of seeing.

The Pharisees, vigilant in the defense of their conception of righteousness, came down from Jerusalem to Galilee to keep an eye on this Jesus, this upstart prophet (Mark 7:1–23). When they saw that "some of his disciples" ate their bread with unwashed hands, they were shocked beyond measure. The sin consisted in a breach of the "traditions of the elders." Righteousness, to the Pharisee, consisted in the correct observance of the traditions, the conventions of religion. If these traditions or conventions contravened the law of God, it was too bad for the law of God. All too often the same spirit has entered the Christian Church.

Sensitivity to the conventionalities of society has always led to the externalizing of religion. To exter-

The Two Minds 149

nalize religious practice is to destroy its power. What went into a man's stomach was, religiously, more important to the Pharisee than what came out of his heart. How the water is applied in baptism is far more important to some Christians than whether the Spirit of God has a part in baptism. This remark is not directed toward the immersionists alone; I have known some who advocated sprinkling with an almost equal exaggeration of the importance of the method by which the water is applied. I make a plea for the supreme importance of the baptism of the Spirit which accompanies every case of genuine repentance.

We know how difficult it was even for Peter to learn that all foods were religiously clean. There was an equal difficulty for Jewish Christians in understanding how circumcision was set aside. It was no easy transition to move from a ritualistic religion to one where only spiritual values are important.

Such a parable as that of the New Wine in Old Wine-Skins (Mark 2:22) was an effort on the part of Jesus to show that what he offered was something new, filled with ferment. Therefore, the old forms could not contain it. The parable of the Patched Garment (Mark 2:21) taught that worn-out Judaism could not be patched up with fragments of Christian teaching without destruction to both.

There must be a sharp break between the new and

the old, because they are hopelessly different. A religion of externalism presents an irresistible temptation to observe the forms of religion to be seen of men. Inevitably, religious life becomes shallow and unreal under such conditions: men become play actors, hypocrites. And yet with the unreality there often goes a fanatical fidelity to forms, to slogans, to shibboleths — a zeal for God which is not according to (full) knowledge: a zeal for righteousness which persecutes the Church. The clash between these two ideas of religion became very violent in the Apostolic Church. In succeeding centuries it has frequently been devastatingly violent in the Church.

Quite unconsciously, the legalist becomes, to himself, religiously more important than God. Returning to the words of the parable, when he prays, he prays " thus with himself "; the Greek says, " To himself," not to God. The mood and emphasis of such a man's prayer is wrong. Its point of reference is all wrong; he thanks God that he is not as other men, instead of acknowledging that he, like other men, is a sinner, needing God's mercy.

Paul had known, as intimately as any man could, what this religion of convention and tradition could do *for* a man and *to* a man. It could make him exceedingly zealous for the traditions of his fathers (Gal. 1:14), but leave him an angry, fuming fanatic (Acts 9:1), kicking against the goad (Acts 26:14), frustrated and seeking to overcome his sense of frustration by more intense persecution. It had made him hard and pitiless as he strove to make men blaspheme and deny their Lord, as he hounded them to foreign cities. It enabled him to stand haughtily by as the dying Stephen prayed, "Lord, lay not this sin to their charge" (Acts 7:60). As Paul recalled these days, he felt that they disqualified him, forever, for being an apostle, except for the grace of God (I Cor. 15:9, 10; Eph. 3:8).

A man "exceedingly mad" against all who differ with him is not likely to exemplify the mind of Christ. It is the way of man to be more intolerant than God. "There's a wideness in God's mercy" which only the mind of Christ understands. The disciples encountered this difference between themselves and Jesus. As we have noticed before, even John fell into this false attitude: "Teacher, we saw one casting out demons in thy name; and we forbade him, because he followed not us. But Jesus said, Forbid him not: for there is no man who shall do a mighty work in my name, and be able quickly to speak evil of me. For he that is not against us is for us" (Mark 9:38-40). For Jesus, the test was, "Does the man do a mighty (good) work in my name?"; for John, it was, "Does he follow us?" The mind of the flesh was asserting itself in John.

But there was need for repentance on other occasions, e.g., when James and John are said to have asked Jesus' approval for calling down fire from heaven on a Samaritan village which did not receive him. "But he turned, and rebuked them. And they went to another village" (Luke 9:55, 56). Codex Bezae reads: "But he turned and rebuked them and said, Ye know not what manner of spirit ye are of." Whether this addition belongs in the text or not, it supplies the point of distinction between the mind of Christ and the mind of two of his closest followers: they were of a *different spirit*. Jesus would leave those who rejected him — possibly another day they would believe; James and John would destroy them. This is merely another example of men of violence wresting the Kingdom to their own standard. It is another evidence of the need for repentance, even in James and John. The achievement of repentance is marked by the two epithets applied to John: "Son of Thunder" and "Apostle of Love." They indicate a genuine reorientation.

Paul, who well knew the spirit that assumed personal righteousness and set all other men at nought (Luke 18:9), could look back on the old life with very clear eyes. He had, as we have noticed before, enjoyed as many religious privileges as any living man — yea, more than most of them: "circumcised the eighth day," and therefore neither an Edomite nor a proselyte; " of the stock of Israel," and therefore one of the covenant people; " of the tribe of Benjamin," and therefore not guilty in his ancestry of revolt against the house of David; " a Hebrew of Hebrews," and therefore not a Hellenistic Jew who had forsaken the language of the fathers; " as touching the law, a Pharisee," and therefore one of the strictest observers of the law; " as touching zeal, persecuting the church," and therefore more loyal to the faith of the fathers than many; " as touching the righteousness which is in the law, found blameless " (Phil. 3:5, 6). But these qualifications had not made him acceptable to God.

To repeat, all these assets, so important in the old religion, he now saw as liabilities: " Yea verily, and I count all things to be loss for the excellency of the knowledge of Christ Jesus my Lord: for whom I suffered the loss of all things, and do count them but refuse, that I may gain Christ, and be found in him, not having a righteousness of mine own, even that which is of the law, but that which is through faith in Christ, the righteousness which is from God by faith " (Phil. 3:8, 9). All his personal achievements in piety Paul now saw as spiritual liabilities, as refuse, for they kept him from gaining Christ and being found in him — in spite of the fact that he had advanced so far in the religion of his fathers (Gal. 1:14).

To be found in Christ meant that he was a new creature (II Cor. 5:17). Having a righteousness of his own — self-righteousness — kept him from having the righteousness which is a gift from God and which comes through faith in Christ. These things put him in that class of whom Jesus said, "I came not to call the righteous, but sinners" (Matt. 9:13). They put him in a class with those who thank God that they are not as other men are and then go down to their houses unjustified.

Paul made the supreme sacrifice of all these things that he might " know him, and the power of his resurrection, and the fellowship of his sufferings, becoming conformed unto his death; if by any means " he might " attain unto the resurrection from the dead " (Phil. 3:10, 11). This is the supreme example of repentance in Christian history. Paul was very near the mind of Christ, and yet was not quite there: "Not that I have already obtained, or am already made perfect: but I press on, if so be that I may lay hold on that for which also I was laid hold on by Christ Jesus. Brethren, I count not myself yet to have laid hold: but one thing I do, forgetting the things which are behind, and stretching forward to the things which are before, I press on toward the goal unto the prize of the high calling of God in Christ Jesus" (Phil. 3:12–14).

This is the man who tells us that the mind of the flesh is hostility to God, that it can never please God.

The Two Minds

This is the man who told the Philippian Christians that they should have the mind which was also in Christ Jesus. He used a present imperative, φρονεῖτε: they must keep on thinking as Christ did. Repentance, the transition from the mind of the flesh to the mind of Christ, is cumulative, and lifelong, and should be constantly progressing. In the thought of Calvin, repentance ought to extend throughout his (the Christian's) whole life.[59] Repentance, as a transition from the mind of the flesh to the mind of Christ, has direction, progress, and destination. If there is a lack of definiteness in any of the three, our repentance is defective.

It is only as we move closer to the mind of Christ that the clash between our wills and the will of Christ is progressively eliminated. At the same time, the conflict within our own beings is reduced. Then Jesus' promise, "Peace I leave with you; my peace I give unto you" (John 14:27), may become a reality.

And be not fashioned according to this world: but be ye transformed by the renewing of your mind, that ye may prove what is the good and acceptable and perfect will of God. — Rom. 12:2.

5

HOW REPENTANCE IS PRODUCED

How does one produce the transition from the mind of the flesh to the mind of Christ which we call repentance? There have been many methods tried by the Church.

The motive of fear has been quite dominant, especially fear of punishment for sin. So prominent has this emphasis been that we find Christians thinking of salvation primarily in terms of escape from punishment in the next world. This is, of course, a pitifully inadequate notion of the Christian concept of salvation, with its abundant life beginning here and now. The Johannine idea of eternal life as a present fact with the Christian and the Pauline idea of the earnest of our inheritance introduce one to reaches of thought that never dawn on the Christian who is moved chiefly by fear.

Persecution and inquisition have been used to bring men into the Church — as well as to drive them out of its bosom. Charlemagne's forcible baptism of the Saxons is not an isolated incident in Church history. All such efforts have brought into the Church men who have not understood or sympathized with the Christian faith. This has always resulted in the undoing of the Church. The fact of having undergone the external rite of baptism gives such converts a sense of having complied with the demands of the Christian faith, without having the remotest idea of what real Christianity is.

How Repentance Is Not Produced

The New Testament has a good deal to say about what produces repentance — and what does not. We shall look first at what does *not* produce repentance.

Fear or Intimidation

Repentance is not produced by the Carolingian method of force or intimidation. Even when the four angels bound at the great river Euphrates had been loosed and had slain the third part of mankind, a slaughter which makes Charlemagne's slaughter of the Saxons infinitesimal, " the rest of mankind, who were not killed with these plagues, repented not of the works of their hands, that they should not worship demons, and the idols of gold, and of silver, and of brass, and of stone, and of wood; which can neither see, nor hear, nor walk: and they repented not of their

How Repentance Is Produced

murders, nor of their sorceries, nor of their fornication, nor of their thefts" (Rev. 9:20, 21).

It has ever been the temptation of religious men to call down fire from heaven on the head of evildoers, but this passage in Revelation paints a picture far more terrible than any fire from heaven that men might call down. The arresting fact is that mankind is still impenitent. "Vengeance belongeth unto me; I will recompense, saith the Lord" (Rom. 12:19). Plagues and suffering do not produce repentance, but it is the goodness of God that leads men to repentance (Rom. 2:4). God does not save men by intimidation and terror, but by love and grace. We should follow in his train, preaching his infinite grace.

When the fourth angel of the Apocalypse poured out his bowl of wrath upon the sun, so that it was given power to scorch men with fire, and men were scorched with great heat, they blasphemed the name of God, but did not repent (Rev. 16:8, 9). When the fifth angel " poured out his bowl upon the throne of the beast; and his kingdom was darkened; and they gnawed their tongues for pain," they blasphemed the name of the God of heaven because of their pains and their sores, but did not repent of their works (Rev. 16:10, 11). Physical pain and anguish may produce blasphemy, but not repentance.

If the aim of repentance were merely to produce

regret for sin, probably plagues and tortures, terror and anguish, would be most effective. A man might bitterly rue the sin that brought the wrath of a vindictive God down upon his head, and at the same time blaspheme, as did the men of the Apocalypse, against the God who inflicts the suffering. A criminal may regret the crime that has put him in the hands of the police — at least he regrets getting caught — and at the same time may resolve to shoot, at his first opportunity, the man who apprehended him in his guilt. But the aim of New Testament repentance is to produce a regenerated mind, heart, and will. Truly, it is the goodness of God that breaks down a man's resistance to grace and melts his heart by kindness.

Increased Evidence

A simple increase in evidence does not produce repentance. When the rich man in torment lifted up his eyes and saw Abraham with Lazarus in his bosom, he cried first for mercy to himself, asking that Lazarus should be sent to dip the tip of his finger in water to cool his parched tongue. It is interesting that Dives could still think of a poor man only in the capacity of ministering to his comfort. A poor man was not his brother, but his servant, even after the balances had tipped decidedly in Lazarus' favor.

When Dives' request for himself was denied, he then

How Repentance Is Produced

thought of his family, but not beyond the family circle of course: "I pray thee therefore, father, that thou wouldest send him to my father's house; for I have five brethren; that he may testify unto them, lest they also come into this place of torment. But Abraham saith, They have Moses and the prophets; let them hear them. And he said, Nay, father Abraham: but if one go to them from the dead, they will repent. And he said unto him, If they hear not Moses and the prophets, neither will they be persuaded, if one rise from the dead" (Luke 16:27–31). A disposition to unbelief is not overcome by overwhelming evidence, even the evidence which a man risen from the dead could offer.

This story of the Rich Man and Lazarus does not stand alone in teaching that more light does not necessarily produce more belief. We find Jesus saying to his Jewish opponents, "Think not that I will accuse you to the Father: there is one that accuseth you, even Moses. . . . For if ye believed Moses, ye would believe me; for he wrote of me. But if ye believe not his writings, how shall ye believe my words?" (John 5:45–47.) A change of *disposition* is required before men can believe.

The specific trouble with this group of Jesus' critics was that they sought glory one from another, and the glory that comes from God they did not seek (John 5:44). All their religious practices were designed to be "seen of men." Although they had a zeal for God, they were so consumed with the task of establishing, i.e., demonstrating, their own righteousness that they never submitted themselves to the righteousness of God — and never comprehended it. This would indicate that the primary barrier to repentance is self-importance. If one's own self-esteem is more important than God's glory or God's approval, one will always be found fighting against God, regardless of one's misguided zeal for God.

Sorrow for Sin

To go into more detail regarding what has been previously suggested, repentance is not produced by sorrow for sin. Judas Iscariot said, "I have sinned in that I betrayed innocent blood. . . . And he went away and hanged himself" (Matt. 27:4, 5). In his case, sorrow for sin led to suicide, not to repentance.

In Esau's case, the loss of his birthright produced intense weeping, but he was still rejected, although he sought earnestly to recover his birthright, for "he found no place for a change of mind" (Heb. 12:17). As I have said previously, the majority of commentators refer the clause, "He found no place for a change of mind," to Isaac, and the American Standard Version fixes this interpretation by adding, in italics, "in his father."

How Repentance Is Produced

The Authorized Version is better in that it leaves the matter open, as does the Greek. Goodspeed rightly, I think, refers the repentance to Esau: "For he had no opportunity to repent of what he had done." Moffatt renders the clause: "He got no chance to repent, though he tried for it with tears." Weymouth improves on both Goodspeed and Moffatt with: "He found no opportunity for repentance, though he sought the blessing earnestly with tears." This is just the point: Esau sought the recovery of his lost birthright and the associated blessing, but *not* the change of mind which would have prevented a resale of the birthright.

Isaac recognized this and refused to undo the bargain that Esau and Jacob had made. The blessing which he bestowed on Esau recognized Esau's ability to appreciate plenty of food and freedom for action:

"Behold, of the fatness of the earth shall be thy dwelling,
And of the dew of heaven from above;
And by thy sword shalt thou live, and thou shalt serve thy brother;
And it shall come to pass, when thou shalt break loose,
That thou shalt shake his yoke from off thy neck" (Gen. 27:39, 40).

Esau wept over his losses, but did not change his mind as to values. A mess of stew was yet to him of more importance than the headship of a clan; therefore he could not be entrusted with the headship of a household, with responsibility for perpetuating the faith of his father.

Esau had forfeited the right and had demonstrated his unfitness for this twofold position. That went to Jacob:

" Let peoples serve thee,
And nations bow down to thee:
Be lord over thy brethren,
And let thy mother's sons bow down to thee "
(Gen. 27:29).

The popular interpretation, which refers the lack of a place of repentance to Isaac, rests upon the mistaken assumption that Esau's copious weeping was itself repentance, and that it would be a contradiction to say that such a man found no place for repentance. Regret over a loss of privilege and repentance, as we have seen, are quite distinct and separate things. In Esau's case, a sense of guilt, mingled with a sense of loss, produced his distress; but both combined did not constitute repentance.

From the account in Genesis, it is evident that Isaac too suffered great emotional strain over the affair be-

How Repentance Is Produced 167

tween his sons, for we are told that "Isaac trembled very exceedingly" (Gen. 27:33). Even though we should refer the clause, "He found no place of repentance," to Isaac, this passage still bears out the New Testament meaning of repentance, μετάνοια. The father, although deeply grieved that his elder son had forfeited his leadership in the family, would not change his mind and put an unworthy son at the head of his household.

But what a picture we get when we refer the clause to Esau! Here was a man crying "with an exceeding great and bitter cry, . . . Bless me, even me also, O my father" (Gen. 27:34); but, basically and essentially, he was the same man who had lightly sold his birthright for a mess of pottage. He was not to be entrusted with the responsibility of administering the heritage from his father, and of carrying on the religious tradition of the family.

"Hast thou but one blessing, my father? bless me, even me also, O my father" (Gen. 27:38), cried Esau, and he "lifted up his voice, and wept." Isaac responded with another blessing, but not the one that Esau had forfeited. So, too, God deals with men, "for he maketh his sun to rise on the evil and the good, and sendeth rain on the just and the unjust" (Matt. 5:45); but he gives the living water, which wells up into everlasting life, only to those who recognize the gift of God and ask for that water which quenches man's thirst for time and eternity. But there must come a change in the man; the natural man gets quite worried when the rains do not come on his crops, but " broken cisterns, that can hold no water " do not worry him in his spiritual life. It is only as the " fountain of living waters " begins to flow that he becomes conscious of the long drought of the heart through which he has lived.

A sense of guilt may cause a man or a multitude to ask, " What shall we do? " But, may I say again, a sense of guilt alone does not necessarily produce repentance. As we have noticed previously, when Peter had finished his great sermon on the Day of Pentecost with the peroration, " Let all the house of Israel therefore know assuredly, that God hath made him both Lord and Christ, this Jesus whom ye crucified " (Acts 2:36), the people were " pricked in their heart." But both the people and Peter recognized that a sense of guilt was not enough, so the people cried out, " Brethren, what shall we do? " Peter replied, " Repent ye, and be baptized every one of you in the name of Jesus Christ unto the remission of your sins; and ye shall receive the gift of the Holy Spirit " (Acts 2:38). Their sense of guilt must be supplemented by faith to produce repentance.

The change of mind demanded here was from that

How Repentance Is Produced 169

of the crowd who cried, " Away with him, away with him, crucify him! " to that of acknowledging Jesus as both Lord and Christ, Sovereign and Messianic Redeemer. This was a hard demand of men to whom the Cross was a stumbling block, but three thousand changed their minds, repented, that day about Jesus of Nazareth. He was no longer, in their eyes, a crucified malefactor, but a sovereign Saviour.

May I repeat that a sense of guilt does not always produce such results. Stephen closed his sermon with: " Ye stiffnecked and uncircumcised in heart and ears, ye do always resist the Holy Spirit: as your fathers did, so do ye. Which of the prophets did not your fathers persecute? and they killed them that showed before of the coming of the Righteous One; of whom ye have now become betrayers and murderers; ye who received the law as it was ordained by angels, and kept it not " (Acts 7: 51–53). These men too were cut to the heart, but instead of asking what they should do " they gnashed on him with their teeth." In this case a sense of guilt drove them mad; they stopped their ears lest they should hear more of that which condemned them; they rushed upon Stephen with one accord and stoned him to death, and cast his bruised and broken body out of the city.

From these two incidents, the conversions on Pentecost and the stoning of Stephen, we learn that a sense of guilt may cause very different reactions. It may lead one man to repentance; it may make another a howling demon, thirsting for the blood of the man who pricked his conscience. It was with such refractory human nature as this that Jesus used the parable so effectively. He punctured a man's self-importance before he could throw up his defenses. The barb of unwelcome truth lodged in the mind to fester and ferment until a response came.

The Apostle Paul gives us a clue to the reason that sorrow for sin does not always lead to repentance: "For godly sorrow [ἡ κατὰ θεὸν λύπη] worketh repentance unto salvation, a repentance which bringeth no regret: but the sorrow of the world [ἡ τοῦ κόσμου λύπη] worketh death" (II Cor. 7:10). According to this passage, sorrow has one of two issues — salvation or death.

The difference lies in the nature of the sorrow. The "sorrow of the world" is without hope and without faith (I Thess. 4:13, 14). It may prompt a man to say, "I have sinned," and then go out and hang himself. But "godly sorrow" is produced by a sense of God's holiness and a belief in his graciousness: again, as Paul said, it is "the goodness of God" that "leadeth thee to repentance" (Rom. 2:4). Godly sorrow prompts a man to pray, "God, be thou merciful to me a [the] sinner" (Luke 18:13): such a man finds peace. But let us recall that this "godly sorrow" is not equivalent to repentance. It merely leads to repentance. As we have noted from Jeremy Taylor, sorrow is the "porch to repentance." Sorrow, coupled with faith in God and a sense of awe in the presence of his holiness, leads to a change of mind; and that leads to salvation, to eternal life. The nearness of the Kingdom is the reason for repentance. We must fall in line with the righteous will of God to share in his reign. Without faith, a sense of guilt leads to despair, to death apart from God. Fright, suffering, and a sense of guilt harden men and drive them from God unless they have trust in his goodness and grace.

How Repentance Is Produced

We now follow Paul's clue: Godly sorrow leads to repentance. Calvin is in line with Paul when he says that repentance follows faith and is produced by it: "Those who imagine that repentance rather precedes faith, than is produced by it, as fruit by a tree, have never been acquainted with its power, and are induced to adopt that sentiment by a very insufficient argument."[60] Again, Calvin says: "Can true repentance exist without faith? Not at all."[61]

The Work of the Holy Spirit

But what produces the faith which produces the repentance? In other words, how is a believing mind related to the Holy Spirit?

In Rom. 12:2 we read, " And be not fashioned according to this world: but be ye transformed by the renewing of your mind, that ye may prove what is the good and acceptable and perfect will of God." This verse is of pivotal importance in our study, for it indicates that transformation of life rests upon the renewing of the mind. This is essentially the doctrine of repentance, couched in other language.

Our next inquiry should be, What or who renews the mind? In this particular context, it is not clear how the mind is renewed, but the matter is not left in doubt in the New Testament. From Eph. 4:17-24, we learn that those who were "darkened in their understanding, alienated from the life of God, because of the ignorance that is in them, because of the hardening of their heart" are to "be renewed in the spirit of . . . [their] mind, and put on the new man, that after God hath been created in righteousness and holiness of truth." Alienation from God is cured by a creative work of God in the mind and heart of man.

From Titus 3:5 it is clear that in this work the Holy Spirit is the creative agent; it is by the washing of re-

How Repentance Is Produced 173

generation and the renewing by the Holy Spirit which God poured out richly through Jesus Christ our Saviour. Here, the three Persons of the Trinity are involved in bringing the estranged mind into harmony with God. It is not done by works of righteousness which we do ourselves. These beget the Pharisaic attitude of boasting: "I am not like other men."

In Col. 3:9, 10, Paul speaks of putting off "the old man with his doings" and putting on "the new man, that is being renewed unto knowledge after the image of him that created him." This is another way of describing the transformation that comes over a Christian during the experience of repentance. Putting off the old man with his deeds and putting on the new is simply another way of saying with John the Baptist, "Bring forth therefore fruits worthy of repentance" (Luke 3:8).

The new man and the new mind are the work of the Holy Spirit. This new man has a new outlook. To him "there cannot be Greek and Jew, circumcision and uncircumcision, barbarian, Scythian, bondman, freeman" (Col. 3:11). All men stand on the same level at the foot of the Cross. All men are the same color under the skin. Racial, social, and cultural distinctions do not count in God's sight, for God is no respecter of persons (Rom. 2:11).

There is evidently a close kinship between the regenerating work of the Holy Spirit and what Paul calls being "in Christ," for he says, "if any man is in Christ, he is a new creature [or, a new creation]: the old things are passed away; behold, they are become new" (II Cor. 5:17). The whole of a man's nature and his viewpoints are changed when a man is in Christ Jesus.

Before leaving Rom. 12:2, we should notice two other very important matters. The first is the contrast between the two verbs "be not fashioned," συνσχηματίζεσθε, and "be ye transformed," μεταμορφοῦσθε. The world, the spirit of the age, fashions men by the external pressure of conventional moralities and entrenched privileges. The spirit of the age is intolerant of nonconformity of thought, of originality, and of prophetic vision. The mood of the age is usually under the dominion of the mind of the flesh; so the regimentation enforced by it is usually crudely materialistic, superficially carnal, and altogether unworthy of man's higher nature.

The transformation by the renewing of the mind describes a change wrought by a power from within one's own being, as an acorn is transformed into an oak. As the life urge within an acorn stimulates, directs, and limits its growth until it unfolds into a magnificent giant of the forest, so the Spirit of God, working on the mind and heart of a man, transforms the mind of

How Repentance Is Produced

the flesh into the mind of Christ. The acorn dies to produce the oak; the old self dies that the new may live. This is repentance — a new mind-set, a new life design.

The second is that the imperative mood in both of these verbs, συνσχηματίζεσθε and μεταμορφοῦσθε, strongly suggests that somehow the human will has a part in this change. This, as we have noticed before, is also borne out by the uniform use of the verb repent in the imperative mood, wherever the context allows. Man is not entirely passive in this transformation. This assumption that the human will plays an important part in reversing one's course of life and thought is also in line with the Old Testament usage of the verb שׁוּב, "Turn ye."

It is further important to notice that these imperatives are usually in the present tense. This serves to remind us that repentance is not limited to a sudden crisis. It is not an emotional cataclysm, but a life process. Repentance in its initial stages is genuine repentance, so far as it has gone, but it must go farther. It is terminated only by death.

A sprouted acorn with only one season's growth to its credit is an oak, but not so large an oak as it will be a century later, when its top towers toward the heavens and its branches reach out toward the horizon. A Christian, just born anew, has something of the mind of Christ and is a Christian, although not grown to the full stature of manhood in Christ. How much Paul insisted on the necessity of growth in the Christian is seen in such passages as: "And he gave some to be apostles; and some, prophets; and some, evangelists; and some, pastors and teachers; for the perfecting of the saints, unto the work of ministering, unto the building up of the body of Christ: till we all attain unto the unity of the faith, and of the knowledge of the Son of God, unto a fullgrown man, unto the measure of the stature of the fulness of Christ" (Eph. 4:11–13). Bringing men to maturity, unto full stature as Christians, is *the* work of the Christian ministry, according to this passage. Maturing in Christian character is concurrent with acquiring the mind of Christ. Repentance and growth in Christian grace should not be identified, but they certainly cannot be isolated, in Christian experience.

To the Galatian Christians, Paul wrote, "My little children, of whom I am again in travail until Christ be formed in you . . . ; for I am perplexed about you" (Gal. 4:19, 20). Paul was in genuine distress because of their obvious immaturity. It was like going through birth pangs again to bring them to a full conception of the Christian faith. How often the conscientious pastor today confronts a similar agony for some of his people!

How Repentance Is Produced 177

All too many of us, both ministers and laymen, are like the scrub oaks of the Coast Ranges of California, which, after fifty years of growth, are more like pea vines than oaks. These scrub oaks often bear a handful of bitter acorns, but they are not very inspiring representatives of the oak family. So, too, Christians may be really Christians, but stunted, scrubby representatives of the Christian family.

The babes in Christ (I Cor. 3: 1-3), who are known by their spirit of jealousy and strife, bring little honor to the Kingdom, and they contribute little power to the Church. They all bear some fruit, but our concern as ministers must be to bring them " unto the measure of the stature of the fulness " of manhood in Christ. The world is crying today for grown-up Christians — grown-up in their emotional and mental attitudes.

Repentance is not fulfilled in sprouting the acorn; nor should it stop when the stature of the scrub oak is reached. It should go on until it reaches full Christian stature, which means that it should go on throughout all of life. When growth ends, death begins.

Scrub oaks usually grow in thin, rocky, dry, and unfavorable soil. A magnificent white oak, rooted in deep soil, with abundant rainfall, is the expression of its favorable environment. The famous Wye Oak,[62] of Talbot County, Maryland, with its girth of twenty-seven feet and eight inches, and a limb spread of one hundred and sixty-five feet, shows us what an oak may be. Few oaks attain such stature, and few Christians attain their full growth, but all Christians ought to be growing.

A man in Christ is rooted and grounded in love (Eph. 3:17), a soil which grows real men. The Christian should not wait for chance showers, but he should ask for the living water which becomes "a well of water springing up unto eternal life." This is the work of the Spirit of God. The Spirit is the agency by which repentance is initiated, carried forward, and completed. Our part is to co-operate. Too often we resist the Holy Spirit of God by which we are sealed.

The purpose of transformation through the renewing of the mind is that we may be able to "prove what is the good and acceptable and perfect will of God." The final goal of transformed thinking is the ability to recognize the will of God in difficult times and situations. Men do not attain this goal by one leap. The Christian advances from insight to insight until he arrives. As he progressively gets the mind of Christ, he will know the will of the Father, for the Father and the Son are *one* in such matters.

Although neither the Gospel nor the Epistles of John use the words repent or repentance, they do

How Repentance Is Produced

have a real contribution to make to our study. This body of literature insists very strongly on the necessity and the consequences of a change in man's inner being.

The Gospel of John, as we have noticed in a previous chapter, calls this change a new birth. With the new birth comes a new nature: "That which is born of the flesh is flesh; and that which is born of the Spirit is spirit" (John 3:6). Since the Kingdom of God is a spiritual reality, it requires a spiritual nature and outlook to understand it or to participate in it. In the words of Paul, "The natural man receiveth not the things of the Spirit of God: for they are foolishness unto him; and he cannot know them, because they are spiritually judged" (I Cor. 2:14).

The First Epistle of John changes the figure, but keeps the idea that the divine activity produces this change in man's moral nature. The phrase "begotten of God" has a dominant place in this Epistle. "If ye know that he is righteous, ye know that every one also that doeth righteousness is begotten of him" (I John 2:29). A change of nature produces a change in conduct. Divine sonship calls for righteous living because God is righteous.

Belief in Jesus Christ is a mark of being "begotten of God": "Whosoever believeth that Jesus is the Christ is begotten of God" (I John 5:1). This test was given by John at a time when men were calling themselves Christians, but not recognizing the Man of Galilee as the Christ come in the flesh: "For many deceivers are gone forth into the world, even they that confess not that Jesus Christ cometh in the flesh" (II John 7). Conversely, belief in Jesus Christ precedes the gift of the Holy Spirit, which produces that revolutionary transformation. It was a group of *believers* who, on Pentecost, were made new men for new tasks. It was to a believing Gentile household that Peter took the Gospel of a Christ "who went about doing good," who was crucified and raised up the third day. "While Peter yet spake these words, the Holy Spirit fell on all them that heard the word" (Acts 10:44).

The book of The Acts does not present one doctrine of conversion while the Johannine literature represents another. They look at repentance in different stages. The work of the Spirit and the response of man cannot be divided into separate compartments that make contact only at one point. There is a constant interaction throughout the entire Christian experience, with the Spirit taking the initiative at every stage.

This divine begetting is the source of Christian love, as well as the source of Christian insight: "Beloved, let us love one another: for love is of God; and every one that loveth is begotten of God, and knoweth God. He that loveth not knoweth not God; for God is love" (I John 4:7, 8). The assumption here seems to be that God cannot impart his life without imparting his nature. Having something of God's own nature enables us to know God. It is a case, again, of the pure in heart seeing God. Likeness of nature produces similarity of taste and sympathy of purpose. Dissimilarity produces a jar, a clash: "And what concord hath Christ with Belial? or what portion hath a believer with an unbeliever? And what agreement hath a temple of God with idols? for we are a temple of the living God; even as God said, I will dwell in them, . . . and I will be their God, and they shall be my people" (II Cor. 6:15, 16). This is another illustration of the need of repentance, reversal of mind. There can be no fellowship with God until it comes.

The divine begetting is also the secret of the Christian's triumphant living: "For whatsoever is begotten of God overcometh the world: and this is the victory that hath overcome the world, even our faith" (I John 5:4). Faith, as well as the Christian, is begotten of God; both are triumphant: "And who is he that overcometh the world, but he that believeth that Jesus is the Son of God" (I John 5:5).

The effect, in the conflict with sin, of this divine begetting is seen in Rom., chs. 7; 8. In the former chapter, all is struggle, agony, frustration, defeat, ending in the despairing cry, "Wretched man that I am! who shall deliver me out of the body of this death?" (Rom. 7:24.) But the light breaks: "I thank God through Jesus Christ our Lord" (Rom. 7:25). The mood becomes one of calm assurance: "There is therefore now no condemnation to them that are in Christ Jesus" (Rom. 8:1). The explanation of the old frustration and agony is the "sin which dwelleth in me" (Rom. 7:17). The secret of the triumph is the indwelling of the Spirit of Him that raised up Jesus from the dead, who shall also make alive our mortal body through his spirit which dwelleth in us (Rom. 8:11). The Christian's hope lies in the creative work of the Holy Spirit which makes the new mind possible. The goodness of God exhibited in the atoning work of Christ leads to repentance. The theologian calls it regeneration. John called it being "begotten of God"; Paul described it as God's Spirit dwelling in us.

But we must not think that Paul (Rom., ch. 8) considered the struggle over. With his mind he still served the law of God; with his flesh, the law of sin (Rom. 7:25). As long as the flesh, the unregenerate nature of man, has any voice in choosing one's course of life, regeneration is not complete. Regeneration is never complete in this life.

How Repentance Is Produced

John was thinking about the ideal when he said, " Whosoever is begotten of God doeth no sin, because his seed abideth in him: and he cannot sin, because he is begotten of God " (I John 3:9). The Church was troubled with antinomian teaching; John replied that there must be a definite break in conduct when a man is begotten of God. He cannot go on sinning.

According to Paul, there are two definite life patterns: the pattern of those who walk " after the flesh " and that of those who walk " after the Spirit " (Rom. 8:5). As there are two patterns of life, so there are two issues of life: " For the mind of the flesh is death; but the mind of the Spirit is life and peace " (Rom. 8:6). Paul spoke first of the Spirit of God dwelling in men and then of the Spirit of Christ, as though they were identical. Manifestly he was wrestling with ideas too big for human speech, but this much is clear: when God comes into a human life, all is different; everything is new. The "man in Christ " has met " God in Christ," reconciling a hostile world to himself through sheer grace — a grace which did not reckon up our trespasses, thus breaking down our resistance to God. Reconciliation is wrought out by means of the message of the Cross. The result is repentance.

In like manner, when one " man in Christ " meets another " man in Christ," even though of a hostile race, the "middle wall of partition" is broken down and the two find a new unity (Eph. 2:14). The barriers erected by race are broken down by means of His broken body, so those who are far off and those who are nigh are made still nearer to God and to one another by one Spirit. A new pattern of life is set, because a new pattern of mind has been discovered.

The Participation of the Human Will

A further word should be said about the part played by the human will in arriving at the new mind. Obviously, Jesus and the apostles, as well as the prophets of the Old Testament, assumed that the will of man plays a decisive part in repentance for, as has been noticed before, the verb μετανοέω is always in the imperative mood, where the context permits such a construction. On the other hand, the verb μεταμέλομαι, which is used of Judas' repentance, never occurs in the imperative mood. In other words, remorse for sin is never commanded in the New Testament.

Remorse for sin may be introductory to genuine repentance, but if the sense of sin does not advance beyond remorse it may be very injurious to the personality. It leads to arrested development of a very unwholesome type, which, in the end, is spiritual death. This is not what Jesus sought when he said, "Repent ye."

As we have said before, nowhere in the Pauline epistles does the writer call directly for repentance in so many words, but the idea is there in other forms. "We are ambassadors therefore on behalf of Christ," said Paul, "as though God were entreating by us: we beseech you on behalf of Christ, be ye reconciled to God" (II Cor. 5:20). Reconciliation brings the hostile mind of the flesh in line with God's gracious purposes. The imperative, "Be ye reconciled," indicates, again, that the will of man has a part in reconciliation, repentance.

Just what part the will of man does play is suggested by the preceding verses: "But all things are of God, who reconciled us to himself through Christ, and gave unto us the ministry of reconciliation; to wit, that God was in Christ reconciling the world unto himself, not reckoning unto them their trespasses, and having committed unto us the word of reconciliation" (II Cor. 5:18, 19). There are several important facts here. The first is that God takes the initiative in this reconciling work, so that man's part consists merely in response to God's approach. It is assumed that man can spurn God's gracious advances, as Paul so vividly reminds us his own people did: "For being ignorant of God's righteousness, and seeking to establish their own, they did not subject themselves to the righteousness of God" (Rom. 10:3). They knew better than God. God was simply wrong about the correct way to attain righteousness.

This conflict between God and his people runs through most of the New Testament and makes a study of absorbing interest. The spirit of contending against God's purpose appears in the words of the Sanhedrin: "What shall we do to these men? for that indeed a notable miracle hath been wrought through them, is manifest to all that dwell in Jerusalem; and we cannot deny it. But that it spread no further among the people, let us threaten them, that they speak henceforth to no man in this name. And they called them, and charged them not to speak at all nor teach in the name of Jesus" (Acts 4:16–18). Peter and John recognized this opposition to God for what it was, and challenged the Sanhedrin with the following words: "Whether it is right in the sight of God to hearken unto you rather than unto God, judge ye: for we cannot but speak the things which we saw and heard" (Acts 4:19, 20).

A second very important fact is the method by which God works out reconciliation. He does it through Christ and his Cross. Jesus completely identified himself with our sin that we might become identified with him in righteousness: "Him who knew no sin he made to be sin on our behalf; that we might become the righteousness of God in him" (II Cor. 5:21). But this was made effective to us by "not reckoning" our sins unto us. As a matter of pure grace, God refused to take account of our sins. Under the Old Testament figures, God removed our sins or covered them; in the New Testament he forgives them. To use Paul's favorite word, God "graces away," χαρίζεται, sin. Reconciliation with God, one aspect of repentance, is made possible because God takes the initiative in graciously removing sin as a barrier to fellowship with himself. This goodness of God leads man to repentance.

A third fact of great practical importance is that God uses human agents in the work of reconciliation: he "committed unto us the word of reconciliation," the Gospel of a crucified Saviour; and he sends us forth as his ambassadors, pleading with men to accept his grace.

Somehow, a creative activity of God works through the message of a crucified Saviour, preached by sinning men to a world in sin and revolt, and so God changes the minds of men from the mind of the flesh to the mind of Christ. This is too wonderful to understand, but we see it operate wherever a crucified Saviour is presented by men who have experienced his grace. God provides the initiative, the dynamic, and the means; man responds; and repentance is the result.

The Powers of the New Mind

The renewed mind possesses not only powers that lead to life and peace, but also endowments for service in the Kingdom. Among these powers are prophecy, discerning of spirits, the interpretation of tongues, and so forth (I Cor., ch. 12). The new mind produces a spirit of wisdom and revelation; it enlightens the eyes of the heart that we may know the "hope of his calling, . . . the riches of the glory of his inheritance in the saints, and . . . the exceeding greatness of his power to us-ward who believe." In other words, the new mind is equipment to live, effectively and fully, for Christ. That is why Jesus said, "Repent ye; for the kingdom of heaven is at hand." No man is prepared to live under God's reign until he gets the new mind.

As John the Baptist expected fruit worthy of the new mind, so did Jesus and the apostles. We catch a hint of what this fruit is in the words of Paul to which we have referred before: "But the fruit of the Spirit is love, joy, peace, longsuffering, kindness, goodness, faithfulness, meekness, self-control" (Gal. 5:22, 23).

The mind of Christ is produced in the Christian by the work of the Spirit. Not only does it bear much fruit, but it sustains the Christian under trial and hardship: "Wherefore we faint not; but though our outward man is decaying, yet our inward man is renewed day by day" (II Cor. 4:16). Our world is calling for men of renewed mind to lead it through the dark days ahead. They must be men who can see God's will clearly and forget their own selfish interests. They must tower toward heaven, spiritually, and reach far toward the horizon in helpfulness to man.

Repentance is produced as the Holy Spirit works within the human life, transforming its aspirations, ideals, ambitions, and viewpoints. The central theme upon which the Spirit plays is the message of a crucified Saviour. The response to this infinite love is repentance.

For though we walk in the flesh, we do not war according to the flesh (for the weapons of our warfare are not of the flesh, but mighty before God to the casting down of strongholds); casting down imaginations, and every high thing that is exalted against the knowledge of God, and bringing every thought into captivity to the obedience of Christ; and being in readiness to avenge all disobedience, when your obedience shall be made full. — II Cor. 10:3–6.

6

THE MEANING OF THESE THINGS FOR PREACHING

The Church must redefine its task. We have had too much preaching that dealt out mild homeopathic doses of ethical exhortation or sought to establish a social utopia by ignoring the fundamental need for a complete change in the mind and heart of mankind.

Jesus and John, as we have noticed, began with this need. The Kingdom was at hand, they proclaimed, and that called for a complete metamorphosis of the mind of man. Like Nicodemus, too many of us have assumed that we are ready to enjoy the benefits of the Kingdom, that we are merely waiting with pious resignation for God to establish it for our especial benefit. The words of Jesus challenge our smugness, as they did that of Nicodemus: "Except ye be 'born anew,' ye cannot enter the Kingdom, ye cannot understand it."

The Apostle Paul reminds us that our task is to capture the mind of man. This includes the subconscious mind, whatever that is. The Church must be told that becoming a Christian requires a new set of values, a new pattern for life, a new mind. If one's thoughts begin and end with one's personal convenience and desires, one is disqualified for Christian living. The preacher must keep reminding the Church that it must become Christian in its ideals, its desires, and its aspirations before it can become Christian in its practice, for the conduct of man hinges on his thought life. A pagan bent in one's thoughts gives a pagan tilt to one's life.

The prophets were the forerunners of John, Jesus, and Paul in relating the mind of man to the practices of man. We have noted before how Isaiah reminded his generation that their ways did not correspond with God's ways, because their thoughts did not correspond with God's thoughts.

As we preach we cannot escape the obligation to remind our people that they cannot build a Christian character or a Christian civilization on a foundation of pagan thought. The attempt to do this has been tragically widespread and distressingly persistent.

The Apostle Paul recognized the crux of his difficulty in the turbulent, faultfinding Corinthian church as lying in the mind of the church members. To make his meaning vivid, he uses a military metaphor to describe his ministry: " For though we walk in the flesh, we do not war according to the flesh (for the weapons of our warfare are not of the flesh, but mighty before

The Meaning for Preaching

God to the casting down of strongholds); casting down imaginations, and every high thing that is exalted against the knowledge of God, and bringing every thought into captivity to the obedience of Christ; and being in readiness to avenge all disobedience, when your obedience shall be made full" (II Cor. 10:3-6).

Paul's task was to capture strongholds, the imaginations of men hostile to God, and to bring them into captivity to, obedience to, the Christ. Since the mind of the flesh is hostile to God (Rom. 8:7), this assault must be made upon the mind of every unregenerate man. The first concentration of attack should be made on the Church, for the victory is not complete until the whole mind is taken; every thought must be brought into captivity to Christ.

The world in its wisdom often demonstrates its own foolishness. The late Canon Streeter said: " The eighteenth century thought of itself as the age of Reason, the last half of the nineteenth as the age of Reasonableness. The present is coming near to being the age of Unreason." [63] These words were penned before the outbreak of the present devastating war. No doubt if Streeter were living today he would say that we are in the midst of a typhoon of unreason.

Man in his wisdom crucified (I Cor. 2:8) the Lord of glory on Calvary; throughout the centuries since, he has recrucified him (Heb. 6:6). In the warfare between the mind of the flesh and the mind of Christ the people have paid a great price, but their only hope lies in the triumph of the mind of Christ throughout the world. The Christian preacher must carry forward this warfare between the two "minds." The battle began in Eden; it was intensified by Jesus' ministry; and it rages throughout our world. This is your fight and mine, and there can be no neutrals in it.

The stronghold to be taken is egocentricity in religion. Paul calls it "imaginations, and every high thing that is exalted against the knowledge of God." He was probably thinking of those stone fortresses built on the rocky Cilician shores as pirate strongholds. From these, men who defied law and order went forth to prey upon legitimate commerce. Roman soldiers were sent to demolish their strongholds. Probably Paul, during his boyhood, had seen the tumbled ruins left by the Roman battering-rams. He may even have seen the demolition of those strongholds. At any rate, he seized upon the attack and capture of them as typical of his own ministry.

The apostolic warfare had to do with the human mind. As pirates may barricade themselves within strong fortresses, defying the proper authorities, so a man may barricade himself against the authority of God, defending his sense of self-importance against all comers. According to Paul there were three phases to his campaign against such fortresses of self-interest: they must be stormed and taken; captives must be taken; and reserves must be held in readiness for the unexpected. This is a magnificent description of what your ministry and mine should be.

Many of these strongholds are within the Church. The professed friends of the Church build strong defenses around some cherished prerogative or ambition and resist all striving toward the ultimate objective of the Church. As we have noted, Jesus probably had this aspect of the Church's warfare in mind when he said, "From the days of John the Baptist until now the kingdom of heaven suffereth violence, and men of violence take it by force" (Matt. 11:12). The Church has never ceased to suffer thus.

Christian leaders today are becoming increasingly aware of the fact that we have dealt violence to the Kingdom idea, trying to mold it into patterns congenial to our prepossessions. Dr. John A. Mackay has written: "We must recognize that in one way or another, Europe, despite its noble Christian history, has tried more than any other continent to be the patron of Christianity. This was true of the Iberian peoples who de-Christianized Christianity. It is markedly true of the current attempt in the Third Reich to evolve a specifically German version of Christianity."[64] The patron reserves the right to withdraw support from an enterprise when he ceases to approve it.

Jesus never called any such disciples. He said, "No man, having put his hand to the plow, and looking back, is fit for the kingdom of God" (Luke 9:62). Jesus allows no mental reservations in those who follow him. Too many Christians are satisfied with being polite to Jesus. Nicodemus made the same mistake: "Rabbi, we know that thou art a teacher come from God; for no one can do these signs that thou doest, except God be with him" (John 3:2). Jesus brushed aside the compliment with, "Ye must be born anew." Politeness to Christ is not enough; anything less than complete surrender does not satisfy the Christ or the Christian.

Modern Europe is not alone in its guilt of forcing the Christian program into the pattern of its own preconceptions. On virtually every first-century mission field the Gospel suffered violence. In Galatia, circumcision was added to the Gospel as an essential for salvation; in Colossae, Gnostic asceticism gave a twist to the Gospel that degraded Christ and defrauded the believer; in Corinth, Christian liberty was perverted into latitudinarian license. Wherever the stream of the Gospel flows through the human mind, some of the dyestuffs of former religious ideas are taken up to stain the purity of the Gospel.

America has had its full share of guilt in this. We have imported our ideas of mass production into the Church; we measure all things by statistics. But the spiritual quality of our members is far more important than the number on our Church rolls.

The acquisitive instinct of the human race has erected many barriers against the advance of the Kingdom. Men lust and kill and covet; they fight and war, because millions believe that a man's life does consist in the abundance of the things he possesses. Largely because of the inconsistency between the Church's professions and practices, we are witnessing a widespread and conscious repudiation of the Christian ideal. " At this moment a frontal attack is being leveled against Christianity by people who are perfectly aware of its nature, and who regard the Christian religion as a menace to all that they stand for and a bulwark against the sinister designs which they pursue." [65]

This mood of the dictators is nothing new. There is something in it that is native to the unregenerate human heart. Wherever the desires of man conflict with the decrees of God, the strife is hot and strong, until the mind of the flesh is changed into the mind of Christ. Man can always find a way to justify his actions. Frederick the Great is reported to have said, " I take what I want; I can always find some pedant to write a book giving legal or historical grounds for justifying my action."[66] The only remedy for this philosophy is to transmute the desires of men as their minds are transformed. The result is fellowship and co-operation where strife and confusion once reigned.

The modern mood of revolt against God did not burst full-blown without preparation. It had its roots in the theology of the nineteenth century, which found it necessary to "think away"[67] whatever conflicted with its theological presuppositions. When we start "thinking away" the deity of Christ, as Harnack and others did, we end by "thinking away" his authority. When it can be said of scholarship, even with partial truth, "If the facts collide with a theory so much the worse for the facts," man is on his way to an era when he is likely to say, "If ethics collide with desires so much the worse for ethics." We seem to be living in that era today.

"Thinking away" the deity of Christ has been followed by translating away the Christian's cross. A modern translation of the New Testament[68] relieves the Christian of any obligation to bear the cross. Wherever the word, σταυρος, refers to Jesus' cross, it is translated, correctly, "cross"; but, wherever it refers to the Christian's cross, it is rendered "yoke." Thus we read, "If any man will follow me, let him deny himself, and take up his yoke daily, and come with me" (Luke 9:23). There is a vast difference

The Meaning for Preaching

between a *yoke* and a *cross*. The one implies service; the other, death. Taking up one's cross is symbolic of the death of the old, unregenerate self. This was another way of calling for repentance, a reversal of mind.

This phenomenon of translation indicates a temper of mind which is rather prevalent in American Christianity. We keep a cross for the Saviour and, in many cases, glory in his sufferings; but we will have none of it in our own lives. We regard crosses as nice ornaments on our church steeples; gold crosses make rather pretty jewelry. But the cross on Calvary was harsh and cruel; there was no beauty in it that we should desire it in our own lives. Too many of us want a Christianity without personal inconvenience.

When the cross is replaced by a yoke, the yoke may soon become a mere sentimental figure of speech. Sentimentality is not the need of the Church today. We need great convictions, great consecration. Diluted devotion will not enable the Church to survive the testing which lies ahead of it.

If American Christians tend to eliminate the cross from their thinking, there are other Americans who take a further step and shrug off any responsibility for their fellow men. H. L. Mencken, writing on the meaning of life, said: "I have done, in the main, exactly what I wanted to do. Its possible effects on other people have interested me very little. I have not written and published to please other people, but to satisfy myself, just as a cow gives milk, not to profit the dairyman, but to satisfy herself. I like to think that most of my ideas have been sound ones, but I really don't care." [69]

It is not so tragic for one who claims to be quite "devoid" of religion, as does Mr. Mencken, to say that he cares very little how his deeds or writings affect other people. We must admire his frankness, but at the same time suspect that he is not so callous as he asserts he is. It is, however, unmitigated tragedy when those who profess the Christian faith adopt the attitude, usually unconfessed, that the effect of their lives on other people interests them very little. It is false friends, such as these, who have dealt deep wounds to the Church.

There is an undisguised revolt against the Church in many lands today. It is by no means absent from America. To a large extent this revolt grows out of the Church's self-centered obtuseness to its obligations. As Paul said of those who had a "zeal for God, but not according to knowledge" (Rom. 10:2), "The name of God is blasphemed among the Gentiles because of you" (Rom. 2:24), so must we confess that the failures of the Church have often brought reproach upon the name of God. Karl Marx was, in part, right when he said, "Religion is the opiate of the people." But he failed to distinguish between the religion that he knew and real Christianity.

We who believe in the Church are false friends if we do not look fearlessly at its sins. We stand on the verge of a new era. Either the Church will emerge from the present world disaster more glorious, as a body of triumphant believers, or it will emerge discredited. God is seeking to use the ministry to bring about its triumph. Loss of faith is not the world's problem, but perverted faith. Men have surrendered their faith in God for faith in a superrace, or for faith in industrial efficiency.

There has been a great deal of talk about the glory and the power of man. This shallow humanism gave rise to a rather obnoxious self-assertiveness. A distinguished author of many books on the social situation one day lamented to Edward Filene, Boston merchant and philanthropist, "the egotism of this generation, its supreme self-confidence, its arrogance and unmitigated insolence." Mr. Filene is reported to have said: "Don't worry about the egotism of youth. Life will make them humble in due time." Life does have a way of taking the egotism out of us. Someone has sagely observed, "No man is omniscient after he is thirty."

Our mission, however, is not to take the egotism

out of man. Defeat of the will of man is not our object; our supreme task is to capture man for a higher freedom. Egocentricity, self-assertion, swaggering self-assurance are simply endeavors of a rather fearful human being to defend himself. It is the so-called "autonomous self" of man that we seek to take for Christ. This battle is not a skirmish; it is a siege.

The Primacy of Preaching

The "primacy of preaching" as the work of the minister stands out boldly in the New Testament. This preaching is usually associated with teaching. The two are inherently interlocked. The point of emphasis in New Testament preaching is clearly the change of the life design of mankind, passing from the mind of the flesh to the mind of Christ. Should this not suggest a proper objective for our own ministry? Budgets and building programs are necessary parts of the mechanism of the modern Church, but the spiritual quality of the people who make up the Church is its lifeblood.

Every great forward movement in the Church has been accompanied, if not brought about, by great preaching. To be great, preaching need not possess the eloquence of men or angels, but it must have a definite purpose. It was the preaching of Savonarola,

The Meaning for Preaching

Huss, Luther, Calvin, Wesley, and Whitefield that stirred men's consciences and shook society out of its smugness. Each of these men had a consuming purpose and therefore each wielded a tremendous power. Aimless preaching might almost be called a contradiction of terms. It certainly has no place in the Christian program.

Throughout Christian history all great preaching has been strongly doctrinal. At different periods different doctrines have been stressed. This has usually resulted in clarifying and establishing some great doctrine in the mind and teaching of the Church. For instance, the Reformation preachers established for Protestantism the doctrine of justification by faith.

There is a desperate need for the New Testament doctrine of repentance to be presented to our generation. It is the only hope for the ills of our world. It proved adequate for the first century; it is adequate for the twentieth. The people will listen to the New Testament concept of repentance. In fact many are groping toward this idea. A sermon on repentance entitled "Rethinking Our Faith" was preached recently in a college chapel. The father of a senior student came up to the visiting minister and said: "I am a lay preacher in my Church and all my life I have laid great stress on repentance, but I have always had the wrong idea about it. I am no Greek student. In fact I have very little education, but I know that the view you have given us this morning is right. It is so much more worthy than the idea I had. Something tells me that it is bound to be right."

Not since the first century has this doctrine of repentance been widely preached in the New Testament sense. Does this explain the Church's loss of power and spiritual vision? In proportion as the Church has debased the true idea, the Church has become like the world — in some cases worse. Scholars have never let the correct idea of repentance quite die out; it now is the task of the preacher to make this information common property.

There is manifestly a widespread if somewhat vague feeling on the part of many that something is deeply wrong in the Church. There is a tide in the thought life of mankind. No one can fully explain it. In some mysterious way certain great ideas lay hold on men's minds in certain ages. Is this not the Spirit of God arousing his Church to a realistic facing of its status? As in David's day, a voice seems to be saying, "When thou hearest the sound of marching in the tops of the mulberry-trees, . . . then thou shalt bestir thyself" (II Sam. 5:24). The time is ripe to present with clarity and conviction the fundamental challenge of the New Testament, "Repent ye."

Getting the Materials

The pages of the New Testament swarm with material adapted to setting forth the meaning of repentance. The problems dealt with then are the same that the minister faces today. There were false ideas of happiness, wrong patterns for success, perverted ambitions, misguided aspirations, misdirected quests in life, false standards of values, wrongheaded notions of God, pagan ideas of prayer on the part of those who supposed they worshiped the true God, and many other ways in which men missed the mark.

The Beatitudes afford excellent material for teaching the Christian idea of happiness. Probably not more than one of the Beatitudes should be taken at one time for a text, but illustrative material could be drawn from the others, with constant contrast between the world's way to happiness and the Christian way. Christianity does not deny men the right to be happy, but the Christian way to happiness is utterly different from the world's. Jesus said, "Blessed are they that have been persecuted for righteousness' sake" (Matt. 5:10). The world would say, "Blessed (happy) are they who escape all hardship." But Jesus said that the world is wrong, and so does experience. Here the minister would have a great opportunity to interpret some of the deeper laws of man's spiritual nature, showing that the pampered and petted and the self-indulged are often more unhappy than any other class of people.

Every pastor has sooner or later to deal with misguided aspirations. Jesus dealt with these too. Sometimes it was the desire for preferment, for position; sometimes it was an overemphasis on the possession of things. When approached by a man who measured life largely in the terms of possessions, Jesus said, " Take heed, and keep yourselves from all covetousness: for a man's life consisteth not in the abundance of the things which he possesseth " (Luke 12:15). The acquisitive instinct is one of the strongest known to man. In many lives the craving to possess things eclipses all spirituality. The " Christian " who measures everything by the dollar mark is trying to serve both God and mammon.

Jesus' warnings against covetousness are very familiar to the Church, but somehow they are not taken very seriously by many of our Church people. If we could show them that such teaching is part of an integrated whole, with one consuming purpose to change the mind of man, these isolated sayings would take on new meaning. In our preaching we should be prepared to point out that the loss of a sense of proportion comes under the call to repentance.

Closely associated with misguided aspirations are

The Meaning for Preaching

misdirected quests. Jesus found his generation largely concerned with food and clothing. He knew firsthand the problem of providing for the needs of a household; he was no visionary. Anxiety for food and clothing is not restricted to either the rich or the poor. Some families who waste enough to provide well for two or three families are most prone to be "anxious." Preoccupation with the physical is poor soil for Christian culture. Jesus said, "Be not therefore anxious, saying, What shall we eat? or, What shall we drink? or, Wherewithal shall we be clothed? For after all these things do the Gentiles seek; for your heavenly Father knoweth that ye have need of all these things" (Matt. 6:31, 32). These words take on new meaning when we see that they are a part of Jesus' total effort to change the thinking of religious people. The Christian's life quest should be different from that of men without faith: "But seek ye first his kingdom, and his righteousness; and all these things shall be added unto you" (Matt. 6:33). The Christian is not required to have a holy indifference to the needs of the body, but he must learn to put first things first.

Jesus' call for repentance included a revision of our sense of values, a redirecting of the major quest of life. Man is more than an alimentary canal to be fed and watered: he is an immortal soul capable of communion with the infinite, eternal God. Many well-meaning Christian people befog their spiritual life by putting it in the second or third place in their scheme of things. Christians do not grow in grace Topsy-like. If one's immortal soul ever begins to reach "the measure of the stature of the fulness of Christ," one must make the business of being a Christian primary. This is a part of the total call to repentance.

Jesus found a great deal of pseudo prudence in the world. The great business of life was to look out for number one. Men scrambled for the place of greatest honor at banquets. Not so many years ago national officialdom was deeply shaken over the same issue, and yet those involved were professing Christians. After nineteen centuries many of us still have not learned the impropriety of these things. If the Church realized that repentance included a revision of our minds on seeking personal honors, the conduct of Christians might have been more seemly in such matters. It should give us pause to recall that the man who betrayed the Master selected for himself a place of high honor at the Last Supper.

Jesus condemned all scramble for personal recognition. If his followers had fully appreciated his many sayings correcting all ideas of false ambition, there would have been no arguments about who should be greatest in the Kingdom. This might apply to some present-day ecclesiastical politics.

The Meaning for Preaching

The instinct for self-display, for self-advancement, and self-protection is native to the human being. That is why the new mind is necessary. Making self secure is the basic trait in common sense, we say. Self-defense is the first law of life for the jungle, but self-giving is the first law of life in the Kingdom of God. Jesus frequently repeats the idea, "He that would save his life shall lose it." [70] He was correcting a deep-seated error in man's thought. Selfish prudence is pseudo prudence. Like the mirage in the desert, self-seeking leads to death — in this case the death of one's higher self. The wisdom of the world is fatal folly. The preaching of repentance includes setting the thinking of people straight on these things.

The New Testament has a great deal to say about mistaken zeal, or wrongheaded ideas about God. As we have noted, Paul, speaking of his own people, said, "I bear them witness that they have a zeal for God, but not according to knowledge" (Rom. 10:2). The crux of their difficulty was their ignorance of God's righteousness and their determination to exhibit their own. All their righteousness was to be seen of men. Jesus said that religious people should let their light shine so that men would glorify God.

When we seek to exhibit our own righteousness we do not subject ourselves to the righteousness of God (Rom. 10:3). It is men of this type who "take the kingdom by force," who wrest its ideas into unrecognizable form. It was men of this type who crucified the Lord of glory. There is a wistful, autobiographical note in these words of Paul: "They did not subject themselves to the righteousness of God." How well he remembered his perverted ideas of God is seen in his words to Agrippa: "I verily thought with myself that I ought to do many things contrary to the name of Jesus of Nazareth" (Acts 26:9). Paul was a sincere man before his conversion, but his spiritual focus was wrong. Someone has said, "We never sin so grievously as when we sin sincerely." As Paul looked back, all his Pharisaic achievements in self-righteousness were spiritual liabilities. They were all recorded in red.

Many warped ideas of God still appear in the Church to block its work. Fortunate is the congregation that does not have a Diotrophes "who loveth to have the preëminence" (III John 9). He may be in the pulpit or on the session or in the pew — or possibly he may be she. If the implications of repentance are understood, there is a rebuke for such a person on almost every page of the New Testament. Preaching should call these things to the attention of the people.

Jesus mercilessly pilloried those "who trusted in themselves that they were righteous, and set all others at nought" (Luke 18:9). The preacher cannot escape the responsibility of reminding his people that the spirit of self-righteousness is one of their most insidious temptations. We have overlooked the insistent New Testament emphasis on this. For example, most sermons on the parable of the Prodigal Son deal with the gracious love of God or the recovery of the prodigal from the error of his ways, but Jesus is represented by Luke as telling the story to illustrate the ungracious self-righteousness of the " elder brother." The father and the prodigal are used by Jesus as background to set forth the elder brother in his true light. The Church has no greater need than to look at itself honestly. The preacher's task is to help his people do this.

Jesus frequently confronted false ideas of prayer. Some people thought they would be heard for their much speaking; some prayed to be seen of men; some prayed to cover up their rascality; others thought of prayer as wheedling a reluctant God into giving them what they wanted. These false ideas are far too common today. Repentance calls for a revamping of our whole conception of prayer, if we hold any of these unworthy notions. From Jesus' teaching and practice we learn that prayer should consist of praise, submission to the will of God, petition for our daily needs and delivery from temptation, and intercession. Prayer should never be for self-display and it is not designed as a means of changing God's will.

The New Testament abounds in the materials we need to correct the mistaken ideas of man. Repentance is the process of getting these ideas straightened out. Many millions yet think that he is great who "lords it" over others, but Jesus said that he is great who serves. The world has found many euphemisms for its perverted ambitions. In Jesus' day those who "lorded it" over others were called "benefactors," εὐεργέται (cf. Ptolemy Euergetes). The writers of the history of Western civilization have perpetuated these false standards by bestowing the title "the Great" on men who were primarily great killers. Occasionally one with prophetic insight has seen through this false greatness:

"Jesus and Alexander died at thirty-three.
  One lived and died for self; one died for you and me.
  The Greek died on a throne; the Jew died on a cross;
  One's life a triumph seemed; the other but a loss.
  One led vast armies forth; the other walked alone.
  One shed a whole world's blood; the other gave his own.
  One won the world in life and lost it all in death;
  The other lost his life to win the whole world's faith.

"Jesus and Alexander died at thirty-three.
  One died in Babylon; and one on Calvary.
  One gained all for self; and one himself he gave.

The Meaning for Preaching

One conquered every throne; the other every grave.
The one made himself God; the God made himself less;
The one lived but to blast; the other but to bless.
When died the Greek, forever fell his throne of swords;
But Jesus died to live forever Lord of lords.

" Jesus and Alexander died at thirty-three.
The Greek made all men slaves; the Jew made all men free.
One built a throne on blood; the other built on love.
The one was born of earth; the other from above.
The one won all this earth, to lose all earth and heaven;
The other gave up all, that all to him be given.
The Greek forever died; the Jew forever lives.
He loses all who gets; he wins all things who gives." [71]

The time has come to unmask euphemisms, to call things by their right names. Exploitation of the brown man, the black man, or the red man should not be referred to as the " white man's burden." If the Church is to survive the catastrophe of " global war " without being almost hopelessly discredited, it must speak with a clear, sure voice. It must have a message commensurate with the tragedy of our day.

The New Testament message of repentance is adequate and there is no substitute for it. We cannot escape the duty of reminding the Church and the world that a Christian civilization cannot be built on a foundation of pagan ideals and practices.

A weak and watery preaching of the brotherhood of man will not taste well to the men who have gone through the fires of the battlefield. They will spew such a gospel out of their mouths. We must assert that the present breakdown in civilization is due to our own double-dealing, our saying, "Lord, Lord," but not doing the things we profess.

If we preach repentance as a paroxysm of sorrow for our sins, we shall not catch the ear of our generation, except for a passing interest, nor shall we preach New Testament repentance. If we say to our generation that the Christian faith calls for a complete metamorphosis of mind, heart, and will, for a new world outlook, we shall get a hearing from those who think seriously. These are they who will do most to shape the new world. This message turned the world upside down in the first century; it will upset those things that need overturning in the twentieth. It will give Christian people a new sense of the significance of the Christian faith.

We do not need a moratorium on preaching; we need better preaching, more purposeful preaching.

Using the Materials

Before the minister attempts to use the abundant New Testament materials on the implications of repentance, he should clarify his own perspective. He cannot set forth clearly the New Testament idea of repentance after having merely read a book on the subject. He should work carefully through the entire New Testament, watching for those passages that are designed to correct the false ideas of men. This, if thoughtfully done, will prove a rich experience. It can be done without undue labor, and the "busy" pastor has time to do it.

When the minister has a clear picture in his own mind of the New Testament emphasis and the implications of repentance, he is ready to begin to share his discoveries with his people. An effective way would be to plan, for the church as a unit, a Bible-reading program centering around the meaning of repentance for Christian living. If properly led Christian people will read the Bible with real enthusiasm. The primary barrier for many is that they do not understand what they read. It is the minister's responsibility to help the people to understand.

Such a reading program could be introduced with a sermon on the New Testament doctrine of repentance. This sermon could be closed with the challenge to read the New Testament from this viewpoint. The program, planned and publicized in advance, could then be introduced. As the reading program is carried out, the pastor should integrate his preaching with the reading of the congregation. There will be questions about some passages which are not understood. The pastor's sermons can answer many of these. As the sermon unfolds some passage that has caused real perplexity, the congregation will listen with a new intensity. As the people begin to see unsuspected depths in the Bible, they will read with a new avidity.

It would be well to note that most of the New Testament ideas of repentance have their roots in the prophets, that they have flowered in the New Testament, and that they should bear fruit in the Christian's life.

If, for instance, the reading program for the week has included the Sermon on the Mount, the minister may take advantage of the opportunity to interpret to his people the Christian concept of prayer. In preparing this sermon he should not limit himself to the materials in Matt., chs. 6; 7. He should rather take a concordance and make a study of the New Testament teachings on prayer. Then he will come to the pulpit with a better-rounded conception of what the New Testament has to say on the subject.

Such sayings as, "I came not to call the righteous,

The Meaning for Preaching

but sinners" (Matt. 9:13), raise questions for many. This offers the minister a natural opportunity to deal with the sin of self-righteousness. These words of our Lord apply to us all. If minister and people together approach this text, seeking to know what it means for each as a Christian, the minister will not preach in the second person but in the first person plural. The minister's remarks will not be pointed so much at the complacency of his people as at the complacency of Christian people in general, of which he too could be guilty. When pastor and people together examine their hearts honestly, both are benefited. Preaching under such circumstances can be quite plain-spoken without appearing to be an attack on some individual to whom the sermon may be particularly applicable. It is to be hoped that the Holy Spirit will apply the lesson to the heart of such a person so that the significance of repentance may dawn on that soul. A congregation led through a Bible-reading program integrated with preaching of this kind would be greatly blessed. Both pastor and people would be chastened and enriched. It would impress on the minister that he should not say of another, "Thou Pharisee"; that it might be more fitting to say, "This Pharisee."

In Matt. 9:13 also, Jesus quotes Hosea speaking for God, "I desire mercy, and not sacrifice." Such a text would enable the pastor to point out the two great emphases in religion, the ceremonial and the ethical-spiritual. Emphasis on the ceremonial leads invariably to formalism, cold smugness, and indifference to the welfare of others. Emphasis on the ethical-spiritual leads to growth in grace and in love for God and man. Man's emphasis tends always to outer forms — forms of church rites or government, proper religious attire, et cetera. The prophets, the Lord, and his apostles were constantly seeking to correct the thinking of the people on these matters. The pertinence of such a sermon today lies in the fact that the things which divide Christendom frequently have to do with these trivialities. The ecumenical mind is an impossibility when one section of Christendom cannot fellowship with another because of a difference in the form of baptism or a different theory of ordination. The first test in the Early Church was love to the Lord Jesus: "Grace be with all them that love our Lord Jesus Christ with a love incorruptible" (Eph. 6:24); "he shall receive the crown of life, which the Lord promised to them that love him" (James 1:12).[72] A second test was love to God: "If any man loveth God, the same is known by him" (I Cor. 8:3). A third test was love to one's fellow man: "Beloved, let us love one another: for love is of God; and every one that loveth is begotten of God, and knoweth God. He that loveth not knoweth not God; for God is love" (I John 4:7, 8). A fourth test was responsiveness to the Spirit of God: "For as many as are led by the Spirit of God, these are sons of God" (Rom. 8:14). Every New Testament test of Christians lies in the realm of the ethical and spiritual, i.e., all are tests of character in response to the grace of God. If one's ministry is exercised in an area where membership in a certain body or submission to a certain rite is *the* essential, these New Testament tests should enable him to clarify the faith of his people.

The Church should have outgrown these pagan notions. The issue of circumcision as necessary to salvation was settled in the Galatian letter. An intelligent reading of Galatians by the congregation, with a few sound, instructive sermons on the principles involved, would solve the question of sacramentarianism for thoughtful people.

As ministers, we must teach our people to turn to the New Testament for light on religious matters, not to old wives' fables or shallow propaganda. The theory of the Protestant Church is that the common man can be taught to read his Bible understandingly. The time has come when we must say that the Church has misplaced the accent on the doctrine of repentance. Retrospection, regret, remorse for the sins that have brought the catastrophe of "global war" on us will not prevent another even more devastating war in a generation or so. Repentance, in the sense of moving from the mind of the flesh to the mind of Christ, will open up limitless possibilities for international understanding and peace and decency. Pious talk about Christian brotherhood, international good will, and interracial understanding can only make the wrath more terrible when a new day of judgment comes, if we continue to condone exploitation at home or abroad.

The Jesus who taught us to pray: " Thy kingdom come. Thy will be done, as in heaven, so on earth," also said, " Repent ye; for the kingdom of heaven is at hand." Reverse your mind, for the will of God will one day be done on earth. The self-satisfied and self-centered cannot fit into that Kingdom. The pastor should teach his people whenever they recite The Lord's Prayer to ask themselves if they would be at home in the Kingdom. How drastically should we all have to change our life design to feel at home in a world where everyone else did God's will? Repentance calls for this change in each of us.

Summary

When the New Testament calls for repentance it is demanding that we correct all our false notions of prayer, of righteousness, of life's objectives, of God and his Kingdom, of all ambitions and aspirations that are not in harmony with God's will. In other words, repentance is a revamping of the outlook and outreach of all life, the metamorphosis of the whole man. Repentance in the New Testament sense covers conversion, reconciliation, regeneration, sanctification, and ultimate perfection. Conversion is the turning of man to God made possible by the regenerating work of the Holy Spirit. Reconciliation is the restoration of fellowship between sinning man and God. Repentance is the change in man, brought about by the Holy Spirit, which results in his turning to God. Calvin was right in insisting that repentance is never complete in this life; it progresses until the day of death. This progress is sanctification. If the " mind of Christ " can be regarded as moral and spiritual perfection, and if repentance is a pilgrimage from " the mind of the flesh " to " the mind of Christ," then perfection is attained when we reach the goal. The tragedy is that most of us have hardly begun the pilgrimage and none of us are in sight of the goal.

NOTES

NOTES

[1] Martin Dibelius, *The Message of Jesus Christ*, 1939, p. 3.
[2] Archibald T. Robertson, *Word Pictures in the New Testament*, 1930, Vol. I, p. 24.
[3] Aloys H. Dirksen, *The New Testament Concept of Metanoia*, 1932.
[4] *Ibid.*, pp. 31, 57, 99.
[5] *Ibid.*, pp. 79, 80.
[6] John Calvin, *Institutes of the Christian Religion*, 1936, III, iv, 1.
[7] *Ibid.*, III, iv, 1.
[8] *Ibid.*, III, iii, 17.
[9] John A. Bain, *Sören Kierkegaard: His Life and Religious Teaching*, 1935. Walter Lowrie, *Kierkegaard*, 1938.
[10] A.D. 1380.
[11] A.D. 1525–1534.
[12] A.D. 1539.
[13] A.D. 1611.
[14] A.D. 1901.
[15] A.D. 1582.
[16] Dickinson and Higham, *The Hexaglot Bible*.
[17] De Cipriano de Valera, *Antiqua Version*.
[18] George Campbell, *Preliminary Dissertations on the New Testament*, VI, 1.
[19] *Ibid.*, VI, 2.
[20] *Ibid.*, VI, 2.
[21] Tertullian, *Against Marcion*, Book II, Ch. XXIV.
[22] Tertullian, *On Repentance*, Ch. IV.
[23] Lactantius, *The Divine Institutes*, Book VI, Ch. XXIV.
[24] *Resipiscentia*.
[25] A.D. 1557.
[26] John Calvin, *Institutes of the Christian Religion*, 1936, III, iii, 5.
[27] *Ibid.*, III, iii, 9.

[28] *Ibid.*, III, iii, 16.
[29] *Ibid.*, III, iii, 9.
[30] *Ibid.*, III, iii, 1.
[31] Jeremy Taylor, *The Doctrine and Practice of Repentance*, II, i, 7.
[32] *Ibid.*, II, i, 8.
[33] שוב. Compare I Kings 8:47; Ezek. 14:6; 18:30.
[34] Jeremy Taylor, *The Doctrine and Practice of Repentance*, II, i, 5.
[35] George Campbell, *Preliminary Dissertations on the New Testament*, VI, Sec. 10.
[36] *Ibid.*
[37] *Ibid.*, VI, Sec. 7.
[38] Thomas De Quincey, *Autobiographic Sketches*, Vol. I, p. 434.
[39] Treadwell Walden, *The Great Meaning of Metanoia*, p. 5.
[40] Matthew Arnold, *Literature and Dogma*, 1928, p. 174.
[41] A.D. 1881.
[42] Treadwell Walden, *The Great Meaning of Metanoia*, 1896.
[43] A.D. 1926.
[44] James Moulton and George Milligan, *Vocabulary of the Greek Testament*, 1930.
[45] It is not necessary to discuss the historicity of Jonah, either the book or the man, for Jesus treats the preaching as historical. We are studying Jesus' ideas, not the correctness or falsity of them.
[46] In the parallel passage, Matt. 9:13 (A.V.), "to repentance" is omitted in the best MSS.
[47] Jeremy Taylor, *Works*, Vol. VIII, pp. 278, 279.
[48] Arthur T. Cadoux, *The Parables of Jesus, Their Art and Use*, 1931, pp. 16, 17.
[49] Author unknown.
[50] Joseph H. Thayer, *Greek-English Lexicon of the New Testament*.
[51] *Expository Times*, July, 1938.

Notes

⁵² *Ibid.*, February, 1939.
⁵³ Burnett H. Streeter, *God Who Speaks*, 1936, pp. 189, 190.
⁵⁴ *Ibid.*, p. 182.
⁵⁵ Friedrich Nietzsche, *Jenseits Gut und Böse.*
⁵⁶ Compare Rom. 1:18–32 as the expression of the outcome of a mind that has rejected God.
⁵⁷ Rev. George Matheson.
⁵⁸ Author unknown.
⁵⁹ John Calvin, *Institutes of the Christian Religion*, 1936, III, iii, 9.
⁶⁰ *Ibid.*, III, iii, 1.
⁶¹ *Ibid.*, III, iii, 5.
⁶² *Wild Flower*, October, 1940, p. 157.
⁶³ Burnett H. Streeter, *God Who Speaks*, 1936, p. 180.
⁶⁴ John A. Mackay, *A Preface to Christian Theology*, 1941, p. 104.
⁶⁵ *Ibid.*
⁶⁶ Burnett H. Streeter, *God Who Speaks*, 1936, p. 181.
⁶⁷ Adolf Harnack, *Sayings of Jesus*, p. 244.
⁶⁸ Charles C. Torrey, *The Four Gospels: A New Translation*, 1934.
⁶⁹ Will Durant (ed.), *On the Meaning of Life*, 1933, pp. 32, 33.
⁷⁰ Matt. 10:39; 16:25; Mark 8:35; Luke 9:24; 14:26; 17:33; John 12:25; Acts 20:35; compare I Cor. 1:18 to 2:16; et cetera.
⁷¹ Charles Ross Weede.
⁷² Compare James 2:5.

INDEX OF SCRIPTURE REFERENCES

INDEX OF SCRIPTURE REFERENCES

OLD TESTAMENT

Genesis
12:2, 3	III, 84
27:29	V, 166
27:33	I, 33; V, 167
27:34	V, 167
27:38	V, 167
27:39, 40	V, 165

Leviticus
19:12	III, 112
19:18	III, 112

I Kings
8:47	I, 35, n. 33

II Samuel
5:24	VI, 206

Job
1:9–11	IV, 143
42:6	I, 35

Isaiah
55:8	II, 55

Jeremiah
8:6	I, 35

Ezekiel
14:6	I, 35, 40, n. 33
18:30	I, 35, n. 33

Hosea
6:6	III, 107

Jonah
3:4b–10	II, 58

NEW TESTAMENT

Matthew
3:2	I, 15; II, 51
3:3	I, 19; II, 51
3:8–10	II, 52
4:3	IV, 142
4:17	I, 15; II, 54; III, 99
4:19	I, 19
4:23	III, 115
chs. 5 to 7	III, 99
5:3	III, 116
5:10	II, 75; III, 116; VI, 207
5:17	II, 55; III, 107
5:20	I, 46; III, 113
5:21, 22	III, 110
5:27–32	III, 112
5:37	III, 112
5:38–42	III, 112
5:43–45	III, 113
5:45	V, 167
chs. 6; 7	VI, 218
6:2–4	III, 104
6:4, 6, 18	III, 111
6:5–8	III, 105
6:9–13	III, 105
6:16–18	III, 106
6:24	IV, 128
6:31, 32	VI, 209
6:33	VI, 209
7:21	III, 117
8:10	III, 96
8:11, 12	III, 85, 118

Index of Scripture References

9:13	II, n. 46; III, 107; IV, 154; VI, 219 (2)	9:38–40	IV, 151
10:39	VI, n. 70	10:42–45	IV, 128
11:12	III, 119; VI, 197	12:38–40	III, 105
13:31, 32	III, 122	*Luke*	
13:33	III, 122	3:7	I, 20
15:28	III, 96	3:8	I, 26, 38; V, 173
16:22, 23	IV, 136	3:10, 11	II, 53
16:24, 25	IV, 144	3:12, 13	II, 53
16:25	III, 104; IV, 146; VI, n. 70	3:14	II, 53
		4:16–21	III, 116
18:3	I, 46	4:16–30	III, 95
19:25	III, 118	4:22	III, 116
21:23–32	III, 118	4:29	III, 116
21:29	I, 32	5:32	II, 58; IV, 146
21:32	III, 118	9:23	VI, 200
22:1–14	I, 20; III, 85; IV, 139	9:24	IV, 146; VI, n. 70
		9:55, 56	IV, 152
26:39	IV, 142	9:62	VI, 198
27:3–5	I, 30	10:13	II, 57
27:4	I, 25	11:1	III, 105
27:4, 5	V, 164	11:32	II, 57
		12:15	III, 103; VI, 208
Mark		13:1–3	III, 117
1:4	I, 15	13:4	II, 75
2:18–22	III, 106	13:4, 5	III, 117
2:21	IV, 149	13:6–9	II, 52
2:22	IV, 149	14:15–24	III, 119
2:27	III, 108	14:16–24	III, 85
4:26–29	III, 123	14:26	VI, n. 70
6:12	II, 56	15:12	I, 37
7:1–23	IV, 128, 148	15:18, 19	I, 37
8:31	III, 90	16:19–31	II, 53
8:32, 33	IV, 136	16:27–31	V, 163
8:33	III, 90	17:20, 21	III, 121
8:35	II, 59; IV, 146; VI, n. 70	17:33	VI, n. 70
		18:9	IV, 152; VI, 212

18:9–14	III, 105	*Acts*	
18:13	V, 170	1:6	III, 122
18:16	III, 119	1:7, 8	III, 122
18:17	III, 119	2:36	V, 168
18:24, 25	III, 118	2:37–41	I, 30
18:26	III, 118	2:38	II, 62, 63; V, 168
19:10	IV, 146	3:13–16	II, 64
19:11–26	III, 121	3:19	II, 62
22:32	I, 16	3:19, 20	I, 40
24:46, 47	II, 60	3:19–21	II, 65
		4:16–18	V, 186
John		4:19, 20	V, 186
1:7	II, 51	5:30, 31	IV, 130
1:11	IV, 130	5:31	II, 62, 65
1:18	I, 43	5:41	III, 101
1:46	IV, 128	7:51–53	II, 61; IV, 131; V, 169
3:2	IV, 130; VI, 198		
3:3	I, 46; IV, 135	7:60	IV, 151
3:3, 5	IV, 138	8:22	II, 62 (2)
3:5	I, 46	9:1	II, 66; IV, 131, 150
3:6	V, 179	9:20	II, 66
3:10	III, 119	9:22	II, 66
3:16	III, 103; IV, 143	10:28, 29	III, 93
5:17	III, 86	10:34, 35	III, 93
5:44	V, 163	10:44	V, 180
5:45–47	V, 163	11:3	III, 94
6:42	IV, 129	11:12, 15–17	III, 94
7:12	IV, 129	11:18	II, 62; III, 94; IV, 135
7:25–27	IV, 129		
9:1–3	II, 75; III, 117	13:24, 30	II, 68
		17:26–28a	III, 92
9:16	IV, 129	17:29	II, 68
10:10	II, 58; IV, 146	17:30	II, 68; IV, 141
12:25	VI, n. 70	20:18–35	II, 62
14:9	I, 43	20:21	II, 69
14:27	IV, 155	20:35	III, 102; VI, n. 70
15:13	III, 104	22:2	III, 98

22:22	III, 98	*I Corinthians*	
26:9	VI, 212	1:18 to 2:16	VI, n. 70
26:14	IV, 150	1:19	IV, 137
26:19, 20	II, 66	1:21	IV, 137
26:20	II, 70	1:23	IV, 131
26:21	II, 70	1:24	IV, 132, 138
28:22	IV, 136	1:25	IV, 132
		1:30	III, 90; IV, 137
Romans		2:6	IV, 138
1:18–32	IV, n. 56	2:7, 8	IV, 137
2:4	II, 70; V, 161, 170	2:8	VI, 195
2:11	V, 173	2:12	IV, 138
2:13	III, 110	2:14	IV, 138; V, 179
2:24	VI, 202	3:1–3	V, 177
3:29, 30	III, 91	3:19	IV, 137
chs. 7; 8	V, 181	8:3	VI, 220
7:17	V, 182	ch. 12	V, 188
7:24	V, 182	13:4, 5	III, 111
7:25	V, 182 (2)	15:9	I, 27
ch. 8	V, 182	15:9, 10	IV, 151
8:1	V, 182		
8:5	V, 183	*II Corinthians*	
8:6	V, 183	1:12	IV, 137
8:6, 7	IV, 134, 135, 137, 138	4:16	V, 189
8:6–8	II, 71; IV, 140	5:15	IV, 145, 147
8:7	VI, 195	5:16	II, 67
8:11	V, 182	5:17	I, 38; II, 67; IV, 154; V, 174
8:14	VI, 221		
8:27	IV, 135	5:18, 19	V, 185
8:28	III, 90	5:18–20	II, 72
9:1–3	II, 67; III, 98	5:19	II, 71
10:2	VI, 202, 211	5:20	V, 185
10:2, 3	IV, 141	5:21	V, 187
10:3	V, 186; VI, 211	6:15, 16	V, 181
12:2	V, 172, 174	7:8–10	I, 25, 33
12:19	V, 161	7:10	V, 170

Index of Scripture References

10:3–6	VI, 195	II Timothy	
12:21	II, 70	2:25	IV, 135

Galatians
1:14	IV, 150, 153
2:11–14	III, 95
4:19, 20	V, 176
5:19–21	IV, 140
5:22, 23	IV, 140; V, 188

Titus
3:5	V, 172

Hebrews
1:1–3	I, 43
6:1–3	II, 73
6:6	VI, 196
12:17	I, 33; V, 164

Ephesians
2:14	V, 184
3:8	IV, 151
3:17	V, 178
4:11–13	V, 176
4:17–24	V, 172
6:24	VI, 220

James
1:2–12	II, 75
1:12	VI, 220
1:19–27	II, 75
1:27	III, 105
2:1–9	II, 75
2:5	VI, n. 72
2:10–13	II, 75
2:14–26	II, 75
3:15	IV, 139
3:17	IV, 139
4:4–10	II, 76

Philippians
1:21	II, 66; IV, 131
2:4	II, 71
2:5	II, 71
2:5–11	IV, 142
3:4–6	III, 114
3:5, 6	IV, 153
3:7–9	III, 114
3:8, 9	IV, 132, 153
3:10, 11	III, 114; IV, 154
3:12–14	IV, 154
4:4	I, 27

I Peter
3:14	II, 75

II Peter
3:9	II, 74

Colossians
2:23	IV, 137
3:9, 10	V, 173
3:11	III, 87, 98; V, 173

I John
1:6	II, 76
2:4	II, 76
2:9	II, 76
2:22	II, 77

I Thessalonians
4:13, 14	V, 170

Index of Scripture References

2:29	II, 77; V, 179	*III John*	
3:7	II, 76	9	VI, 212
3:9	II, 77; V, 183		
4:7, 8	V, 181; VI, 221	*Revelation*	
4:10	II, 76	2:5	II, 78
4:19, 20	II, 76	2:16	II, 78
5:1	V, 179	2:21, 22	II, 79
5:4	V, 181	3:18, 19	II, 79
5:5	V, 181	3:20	II, 79
		9:20, 21	V, 161
II John		16:8, 9	V, 161
7	V, 180	16:10, 11	V, 161

www.ingramcontent.com/pod-product-compliance
Lightning Source LLC
Chambersburg PA
CBHW070312230426
43663CB00011B/2096